Green is the New Black

Green is the New Black

How to
Change the World
with Style

TAMSIN BLANCHARD

HODDER &
STOUGHTON

2

British Library Cataloguing in Publication Data
A record for this book is available from the British Library

ISBN 978 0340 954300

Printed and bound in Great Britain by
Clays Ltd, St Ives plc

The paper used in this book is a natural recyclable product
made from wood grown in sustainable forests.
The hard coverboard is recycled.

Hodder & Stoughton
A Division of Hodder Headline Ltd
338 Euston Road
London NW1 3BH
www.madaboutbooks.com

Contents

designs from Cast Off, Junky Styling, Antoni & Alison
and many more . . .

Foreword by Lily Cole

I could say shop less. I could say shop here. But I would be an annoying hypocrite, since I shop a lot and buy clothes without reading the labels. I would, however, encourage thrift shopping. I would encourage buying quality over quantity. I would encourage sewing together your own stuff, and keeping that stuff even as it falls apart (a good look, I really believe). I would also encourage a change in attitude. While it is a nice idea that we all boycott 'bad' designers, buy only green etc., etc., the proportion of us willing to do so is VERY marginal. It is an awkward and difficult task.

At a time when we are faced with environmental crisis, when polar caps are melting, sea levels rising, cotton and clothes production are employing child and underpaid labour, and people are producing their body weight in waste every seven weeks, the green movement must address every aspect of the concerned or thoughtful citizen's life, right down to the clothes we wear.

While my job largely prevents me from legitimate preaching, I also happen to know a thing or two about the emptiness of excess shopping. At school, I underlined an Eric Fromm line that struck me: 'greed is a bottomless pit that tires a person trying to satisfy a need without ever reaching satisfaction'. Yep, I can relate. I was once the prototypical material girl. But I went from the little girl who didn't have much and wanted everything, to the girl who would buy piles of stuff and didn't know what to do with it.

As many people are beginning to make ethical choices about their transportation or what they eat, it's funny how few are shopping green for clothes. We may make an effort to ride bikes and buy organic apples from the farmers' market, but rarely do we consider something as simple as the inexpensive socks on our feet.

Not many of us realise that it has likely taken a cupful of unregulated pesticides to produce the cotton in those socks. Nor are we aware of the fact that the cotton may have been picked by underpaid child labourers in Uzbekistan, travelled by ship to Bangladesh, been sewn together by workers getting paid five pence an hour for an eighty-hour week, and then flown around the world once more in a cargo plane to fit our feet for less than a pound – all because we refuse to pay more than two.

Not to mention that most socks aren't designed to last, so we buy seven packets. But no matter, we'll just add our disintegrating, holed pairs to the landfill site at the year's end. The consequences are easy to overlook, buried and forgotten beneath the other one million tonnes of unwanted clothing us Brits have chucked out that year.

I know I risk sounding like a charlatan – the model trying to make you feel guilty for buying clothes while earning her keep by persuading you to buy them in the first place. The truth is, while I've long had misgivings about the industry I work in, it was only when the Environmental Justice Foundation (EJF) approached me last year that I really began to see the global repercussions of the fashion industry.

The EJF handed me a report detailing Uzbekistan's environmental and human rights violations in association with cotton production. Cotton, harmful? Who would have thought? But the report was so overwhelming I was forced to fight back tears while reading it on a train across London. I'd never felt so hypocritical.

I don't do much, and I don't imagine I can do much, but one of the more useful consequences of my role as a model might be to encourage more people to ask questions about the global clothing industry and what we can do to change it. An obvious first step is to demand higher quality and ethics in fashion, just as we've begun to do in other industries.

Company chief executives and storeowners are a pragmatic bunch who live and breathe to expand and protect their revenue streams. By and large, they will be more likely to address the unethical sourcing of their products and consider change if real money is at stake. It's a simple tug-of-war: on one side, most companies try to seduce us into buying lesser-quality products through clever advertising (using humour, models, celebrity endorsements); on the other side, smart consumers pull back by demanding better products or by holding their wallets tight. Capitalism is only as ruthless as its consumers. After all, the customer is king, right?

The second step (my favourite) is to buy and wear more second-hand clothes! As much as I have tempered my shopping blitzkriegs, my appetite for used and second-hand clothing has increased exponentially over the past two years. I react to seeing charity shops or vintage stores these days with the enthusiasm small children reserve for sweetshops. I'm not quite sure why, but I've grown to simply love ragged edges and missing buttons. I enjoy things that way. Like getting a book from a friend, instead of buying it. What's a good pair of shoes without being perfectly worn-in? What's a real jumper without a hole? I've begun to strangely enjoy monthly culls of my wardrobe – giving to charity shops, my family, my girlfriends. Nothing warms my heart more than to see my friend Lorna enjoying a pint in my old striped sailor shirt.

While reports like the one from EJF have helped open my eyes a bit wider, on a different level I've also found myself slowly going back to the way I was brought up. Since we never had much when I was a child, most of my clothes were inherited from my older sister. My mum was the master of creating the new from the old. She would re-tailor pieces to make them fit better or, as I suspect now, in an effort to make me feel I was getting something new and exciting. And whereas I used to burn for the fanciest clothes in the fanciest shops, I now look back fondly at my mum stitching up a torn designer dress I was to wear at a party with parts of my window curtains. I'm reminded of that beautiful Malcolm de Chazal line: 'The idealist walks on tiptoe, the materialist walks on his heels.' I'd like to think I'm relearning how to walk on my tiptoes.

Everything must begin somewhere. How many of us regularly bought organic food ten years ago, let alone had even heard of fair trade clothing three years ago? Enveloped by a new wider consciousness, ethical fashion seems to be a small part of what might be the tipping point, as society comes together to ask for change.

The fact that this book has been put out by a major publishing house and that you are holding it now is proof in itself that these ideas are gathering momentum. Imaginative and well researched, *Green is the New Black* is a resounding clarion call for this new direction in fashion, and I am honoured to have been asked to write the foreword for what I hope will become a bible for the ethical shopper.

So keep asking, keep demanding and keep being concerned. Above all, please keep in mind that we consumers are the kings and queens. If enough people ask, we get. And please remember, or at least consider, that holes can be beautiful too.

Happy shopping!

Lily Cole x

Introduction

To be honest with you, green is not an easy colour to pull off. It's hard to save the world when you're busy travelling round it, on the look-out for the next big thing. As a newspaper fashion editor, I would jet off to Milan at least twice a year, and the same for New York, following the rest of the fashion circus on its quest to see the next season's trends and designs. Then there would be the trip to Tokyo to interview a designer, a visit to São Paulo in search of Brazilian fashion, or a luxury conference in Istanbul. Most big cities host a fashion week these days: Sydney, Moscow (for some reason, it hosts two each season), Athens, Johannesburg, Lisbon, Madrid, Mumbai, Hong Kong, Beijing.

The fashion industry loves to fly – preferably with bags and cases by Louis Vuitton, which, if you are lucky, will be FedExed ahead so you don't have to hang around the luggage conveyor belts. Magazine editors will fly a team halfway round the world to find an exotic location to serve as a backdrop for their glossy fashion stories. Models, it seems, spend more time mid-Atlantic than they do in their own homes. Fashionistas are as profligate with their carbon emissions as they are with their air kisses.

Although I don't travel as much for work these days, I'm not perfect. In fact, I'm not even approaching perfection. My carbon footprint is 3.7 global hectares, or 6.11 tonnes (according to www.rsacarbonlimited.org), which means if everyone lived like me we would need 2.1 planets to sustain our lifestyles. I drive a car – less than 5000 miles a year, but still, I do drive a car. I wish I could drive a cute little electric G-Wiz, like the designers Eley Kishimoto, who have even covered theirs in their own print (see page 189), but by the time I fitted the baby seat and the shopping into it, there wouldn't be any room for me.

Biggest sin of all, of course, is that I'm a material girl. I love clothes. I have always loved clothes. It is my job to write about designers and their latest eccentricities and collections. I actively promote consumerism. I am always on the look-out for what's new. Fashion, by its very nature, is about in-built obsolescence. It's about waste. We fashion people revel in waste. We look disapprovingly at anyone wearing last season's boots. We want everything to be new, new, new. We want it before it is even in the shops. We are already shopping for winter the spring before. We pride ourselves on being ahead of the game. We like nothing more than a nice, shiny (and yes, often plastic) carrier bag, full of new clothes.

The problem is, lately the whole business has started to look kind of ugly . . .

I have been writing about fashion since the early 1990s, around the period when Alexander McQueen and Hussein Chalayan erupted on the London catwalks. At that time, the high street was something that complemented designer fashion. Inspirations undoubtedly filtered down, and you could always 'get the look' for less. But it was a relatively gentle affair. Over the past ten years, however, since the advent of brands like Florence & Fred at Tesco, and George at Asda (the first supermarket brand to launch in 1990), it has become possible to buy pretty good catwalk rip-offs for the price of a pizza, while you do your weekly shop. Everything is up for grabs, whether it is the latest Chloé handbag, or the coolest Marc Jacobs jacket. And, often, the copies are on the shelves before the real thing arrives in the boutiques and department stores – certainly, they come in bigger sizes and huge production runs, so you won't have to join a waiting list.

It has become a form of inverted snobbery to see who can pass off their designer look-alike as a catwalk dream, and then boast that it only cost £3 from Primark. It makes us feel smart, as though we have got one over on the designer brands. And everyone is at it, from teenage schoolgirls to footballers' wives. In her book, *That Extra Half an Inch*, Victoria Beckham boasts about her supermarket buys alongside her Roberto Cavalli and Dolce & Gabbana. Cheap, fast fashion has become as much a part of our celebrity culture as McDonalds cheeseburgers and Starbucks coffee. It's all so tempting, instantly gratifying, and great fun. Fashion magazines from *Vogue* to *Grazia* can't get enough.

There was a time when *Vogue* would never have endorsed companies such as Primark, but now it's simply seen as cheap chic. And why not? The celebrities are wearing it after all! The Sunday supplements promote the ultra cheap too. Rarely a week goes by without a mention of ASOS.com – As Seen On Screen – where you can buy a sequin trim Lurex dress 'in the style of Paris Hilton' for a mere £35. Incidentally, if you click on their organic/fair trade section, you can also buy an 'Organic Lindsay No Worries Sloppy Tee in the style of Lindsay Lohan' for just £20.

We all love to be kept up to date on the latest bargain buys. And what, you may wonder, is wrong with that?

Fashion victims

What's wrong is that, because clothes are so cheap and because Primark is the new Prada, we have started buying more clothes than ever before. Women's clothing sales in Britain rose by 21 per cent between 2001 and 2005 alone, to about £24 billion, spurred by lower prices, and the fact that stores now bring new stock on to the shop floor every month rather than every season. We have become a nation of shopaholics. We love the fact that we can now buy armfuls of clothes – several outfits – for the same price we used to pay for a single item. It is, of course, part of the democratisation of fashion. What was once the preserve of an elite few who could afford it, is now accessible to all – albeit in poor-quality fabrics and badly made, wear-today, throw-away-tomorrow designs.

A Chanel jacket is all about the weight of the chain at the hem of the lining (to make the jacket hang just so) and the quality of the tweed. It will last a lifetime. But an entire generation seems to have forgotten about workmanship and quality. Instead, we want a quick, cheap fix. It's almost better if you haven't splashed out on the real thing, because you can chuck it out and buy a new one when you get bored. Even fashion editors, the sort of people who would never have been seen dead in their local Matalan a few years ago, will go in search of the latest cheap thrill at Primark or Peacocks. The only difference is that they wear it with their Marni and the whole look will take on a postmodern irony.

If you are spending £8 on a jumper, it's worth asking, was the person who made it paid a living wage? I know you love the jumper, and I know it was a bargain, but it is no coincidence that the minimum wage for garment workers in Bangladesh halved in real terms during the 1990s. War on Want's report, *Fashion Victims*, finds that machinists in Bangladesh are receiving as little as £8 a month to produce cheap clothes for British consumers – that's a third of the minimum living wage.

The competition to make ever-cheaper clothes – to feed an increasingly voracious appetite for fast fashion – is fierce. Not only are we producing more clothes than we could possibly need in ten lifetimes, and demanding that they are cheaper and cheaper, we have lost our sense of style in the process.

The charity Traid (Textile Recycling for Aid and International Development) has been noticing a marked increase over the past few years in donations of cheap and cheerful clothing – much of which is donated with the swing tags intact. If a T-shirt cost £2 new, who is going to buy it second-hand and washed up? These are not the hand-me-downs and heirlooms of future generations. We will be lucky if they last the season before falling apart at the seams.

Making the cut

It's time to start asking questions. Here are some for starters. Can I make a difference to people's lives by choosing organic cotton? Should I wear leather if I'm a vegetarian? What's the impact on the environment of leather (all that excess methane) or, for that matter, plastic and synthetic shoes? Of course there is nothing as natural and sustainable as a woolly jumper, but should I be concerned about the practice of mulesing, which involves cruelty to the sheep? Should I wear acrylic instead? It'll cut down on washing and aftercare and it takes a shorter time to dry, which means lower carbon emissions. You might be worrying about the number of plastic bags we accumulate in a single day's shopping. You might begin questioning the sheer volume of clothes we are buying at knockdown prices. Are we contributing to the world's mountain of waste? And who exactly is paying the price for our bargain catwalk rip-offs?

Of course, the closer you look, the more complex the picture. Shopping can seem like an ethical minefield these days. For example, a T-shirt bearing the now highly recognisable Fairtrade logo might only be made using Fairtrade cotton. The T-shirt itself might have been sewn together in a sweatshop in the Far East and been flown halfway across the world for distribution. The cotton, while grown by farmers who are paid a living wage, might have been produced using pesticides that are harmful both to the environment and the farmer and his family. In America, fashion designers who attempt to make sustainable clothing using fair trade practices don't describe themselves as 'ethical', since the implication is that the rest of the industry is unethical. Now this may be the case, but nobody wants to start a lawsuit.

One of fashion's thinkers, Hussein Chalayan, explains the problem: 'It is hard to engage with the full picture. You can buy a fabric that is carefully produced but you can't control it at every stage. Designers are depending on their producers who get their supplies from elsewhere. There's not enough information about. I'd love to know the greenhouse emissions caused by the production of a single jacket but I can't find that out. Also, as designers, we have to fly a lot. So any gains you make by using an organic fabric are undone by a single flight. There are lots of knock-on effects and things cancel themselves out. On average, I take about ten flights a year, mainly between London and Italy and Istanbul. I usually fly to America once a year. There needs to be a more deep-rooted solution to how things are produced.'

Thankfully, because more and more of us are asking questions – and demanding answers – the ethical clothing movement is gaining momentum. The industry is listening to our concerns and has started cleaning up its act. Companies like Marks & Spencer are going full speed ahead to change the way they work, with their aim to be carbon neutral by 2012. The first eco factory opens in Sri Lanka in 2007. The rest of the British high street is racing to keep up. H&M has launched its first organic cotton range, as has New Look, Dorothy Perkins and Primark. Sainsbury's has launched Fairtrade cotton basics. Topshop is learning from its work with the Fair Trade label People Tree, and investing in cotton at the seed stage, to ensure that it is fairly traded at every step of the way.

Thanks to the savvy consumer, and many of the designers, models and style icons featured in (and contributing to) this book, this season it's perfectly possible to combine high principles with high fashion, in all its high-heels-wearing, trends-frenzied, air-kissing glory.

Closet confession

My own ethical epiphany happened on the hottest day of the year in the summer of 2006. I was helping to create a 'farmers' market of fashion' as part of the Hackney Empire's annual Spice Festival. It seemed fitting that there should be an eco theme to the day – many of the designers were using sustainable fabrics or recycling old clothes. We were promoting local produce from local designers and craftspeople so 'fashion miles' were kept to a minimum.

The campaign group Anti-Apathy and their flame-haired founder Cyndi Rhoades had come along to spread the word about 'change through lifestyle'. Which meant that in the middle of the chaos and the heat was a strange sight: their 'Earthly Sins Confessional Booth', looking as though it had fallen out of the sky like Dr Who's Tardis and on to the grass by Hackney Town Hall. Taking her booth to workshops and festivals around the country, Cyndi encourages those who dare to sit and confess their fashion sins. It's a great starting point for advice and debate on sustainable style.

I ventured inside, not knowing what to expect, save at least ten Hail Marys and a couple of Our Fathers. At first glance, I didn't fare too badly. I tend to wear clothes over and over again, so Cyndi was lenient about my Eley Kishimoto print smock, now well into its third summer and my seriously ancient (and faded) trousers – Martin Margiela 6, from years ago. As the session progressed, however, my green goddess credentials began to pale. Pushed to account for my wardrobe's contents, it became apparent that I had no idea what I owned – apart from a complete lack of Fairtrade and organic logos and, it seemed, far too many clothes.

And so, I went home that night and embarked on a closet clear-out to make my mentor proud. I was shocked, and a little embarrassed, to discover at least two pairs of black trousers that I had never hemmed and hence never worn. One still had the swing tags on. They'd been hanging there for months. An entire season! Black trousers are always useful, of course, but why was I still shopping for them? All I needed was to get the sewing machine out and, hey presto, two new pairs without so much as a queue at the till.

Three bin-bags of clothes, shoes and It Bags later and I had some real gems to recycle, swap and sell (see page 28). These included: a ten-year-old Givenchy coat (the most expensive item I've ever bought – well, almost – and now tragically worn at the edges); a Miu Miu skirt; a few cashmere jumpers (moth-eaten); a Paul Smith blouse (barely worn); a Clements Ribeiro raw silk tunic (well worn, but too small); plus some other bits from Gap, Muji, Zara and French Connection.

Which left me with forty-one dresses. I know, I know, who needs forty-one dresses? But something had to give. And, audit done, I had, at least, resolved to swot up on more sustainable style options before buying dress number forty-two.

Thus my quest to become an ethical fashionista, something I had toyed with for years, but never seriously implemented, had properly begun.

If style is ultimately about self-expression, ethical fashion is increasingly the place to find it. It's all about the joy of dressing up, discovering new fabrics, dyeing your own, being more resourceful, or simply having fun with a ball of wool. It feels to me more like the 1980s, when style was essentially finding vintage clothes, making your own or customising what you had. I look back at my old copies of *i-D* magazine and while the clothes might look a little odd in retrospect, they were all about individuality and creativity.

As I have found, and as you'll see in the following chapters, there's so much on offer today it's easy to make the right choices. Things are changing. And in fashion, change tends to happen at a fast pace. Who knows, if you are walking round in your alpaca Ciel legwarmers, your Beyond Skin vintage heels, and your customised, recycled Junky Styling shirt-dress (get the low-down on these later), you might just be starting something. Designers have spies everywhere. Your look could become their look on a catwalk near you soon.

At the very least, I hope that this book will show you how to choose the handbag and the heels that enhance your life, and contribute least to global warming. How to discover the must-have dress that didn't poison farmers with pesticides, force women to work for pennies, or compromise your personal taste. How to refashion your wardrobe and, with it, your way of life . . .

And by putting a bit more thought into what you're buying, and bringing a fresh attitude towards the way you dress, I hope that – like me – you'll reclaim something quite special along the way: your own fabulous look and style.

How to use this book:

At the end of *Green is the New Black*, you will find the Little Green Book. This includes a directory of the very best designers and labels mentioned in the following chapters, a reading list to inspire, fun things to enjoy, and the most useful, informative websites to visit. In case the mood takes you, I've also included a couple of letter templates for you to amend and send. Remember, the consumer is king! So write to your favourite shops and see what you can do to help make a difference.

1

*Getting
the Look*

Getting the Look

*'Fashion is not something that exists in dresses only.
Fashion is in the sky, in the street, fashion has to do with
ideas, the way we live, what is happening'*

Coco Chanel

Changing Fashions

The best fashion reflects the times we live in. It responds to what's happening in music, art, the big exhibition, the latest Hollywood blockbuster and, like a great big sponge, it soaks up everything it touches. The most creative designers are the ones who are most open to what's going on around them. John Galliano has always been inspired by – and in tune with – club culture. Alexander McQueen finds his vision in some obscure film, or in history. Marc Jacobs taps into music and art. Culture, travel, politics, even the stock market can affect how a designer is thinking and, ultimately, what we will be wearing.

It's hardly surprising then that the idea of global warming as an issue has been bubbling away in the fashion subconscious for at least a decade. We've had seasons where it's been all about nature. In fashion terms this will translate into a lot of raffia or linens or floral prints. And it is interesting to see how individual designers respond, whether it is a Stella McCartney jumper with a penguin knitted on to it (was she watching *Happy Feet*?) or Miuccia Prada declaring that she is bored with fashion – too much over-consumption perhaps?

But of course, global warming and sustainable fashion are not simply seasonal trends. They are here to stay. Which means the high street is taking the issues seriously too. And with our favourite chains racing each other to snap up organic cotton or falling over themselves to be branded Fairtrade, it's more important than ever to be selective about where you shop.

Discovering Your Style

As an aspiring green goddess, you should aim to buy pieces that are not going to fall apart after the first wash, or look out of date by the end of the week. If you're not sure about that lime green top with epaulettes, don't buy it. If you have your own personal style, it is not important what is in or out of fashion. If it's part of your particular look, then you will want to wear it for as long as it gives you pleasure.

There are as many ways to look gorgeous, and be ethical, as there are trends in any season. You do not have to conform to a particular look. Just remember:

* You don't have to wear hemp, and if you do, it doesn't have to look like hemp.
* You don't have to wear a slogan on your T-shirt, although slogan T-shirts are in vogue this year.
* You don't have to wear shoes that look like Cornish pasties (though I personally quite like a bit of a Birkenstock).
* You don't have to look like you've been pulled through a hedge backwards.
* You don't have to have lank hair, or shocking pink hair, for that matter.
* You don't have to wear patches on your elbows.
* You don't have to wear shades of sludge.

Of course, if you want to do any of the above, that's fine too. It's your look. Here's where to find it . . .

eBay

Everyone knows an eBay addict, and most of us have tried it at least once. Clothes and shoes make up 11 per cent of the items sold on the site, second only to collectables with 17 per cent of the sales. Auctioning fashion online is a serious business. Even celebrities are hooked. Self-confessed addicts include Sophie Ellis Bextor, whose spending sprees have included a pinball machine as well as endless clothes and accessories. Lindsay Lohan is known to stock up on hats and sunglasses.

Vintage isn't the only fashion fare up for auction. As an attempt to raise its fashion quotient, eBay hired ex-*New York Times* style reporter, Constance White, as its own style director. As well as editing the website's 'personal style' page, White's job is to find designers who want to sell their work for a limited period on eBay. Successes have included the American designers Proenza Schouler.

Celebs don't just use it for boosting their wardrobes; Keira Knightley sold her Vera Wang dress from the 2006 Oscars on eBay for £4301. The proceeds went to Oxfam's £20 million appeal for the humanitarian emergency in East Africa and were enough to feed 5000 children in Tanzania for a month.

A couple of words of warning. Never get into a bidding war after you've had a few glasses of wine. And beware of fakes (see page 203 for more on this).

Charity shops

It is worth shopping around. Although the Notting Hill branch of Oxfam's prices might mirror that of the higher end of the high street, the clothes are more likely to be good quality – and besides, you are giving to a good cause.

Some postcodes still have charity shops full of unearthed goodies. The Cheshire branches of Oxfam are reportedly where the WAGS offload the fruits of their shopping sprees.

As a general rule, head to coastal villages and historical towns. When it comes to finding a Mary Quant original for £1.50 we have to get ruthless.

If you are lucky enough to find a Burberry trench, a YSL tuxedo, a Margaret Howell shirt, or a Ballantyne twin set, then please send me the details of your local charity shop. You obviously live in the right neighbourhood. And I promise, I won't tell a soul.

Things to look out for

* Seventies platforms, 80s court shoes. Generally people's feet have got bigger, so you are more likely to find your new favourite dancing shoes if you have dainty feet. A good cobbler will re-heel stilettos for a couple of pounds.
* 1950s bathing suits.
* Seventies sun hats.
* Anything gold lamé (always handy around Christmas time).
* Scarves, from Scottish shawls to Eley Kishimoto style prints – these can be picked up for a pound or so.
* Belts: elastic waist belts, diamante encrusted, patent, ethnic.
* Handbags, soft quality leather that no one else will have; quirky summer shoppers to stow your knitting on the train. Pearly clutch bags with matching purses inside.
* Costume jewellery, pretty gold chains, and ornate brooches to brighten up a winter coat.
* Cashmere and cosy cricket jumpers. The men's section is great for quality cashmere and angora to hang around the house in, or pull on your vintage belt and wear out with leggings and boots.
* Berets – quality Kangol ones in a colour for every outfit.
* Tailored tweed. One memorable find was a friend's DAKS tweed jacket from an Oxfam in Bath for £4.99. She changed the

buttons to 1960s Bakelite orange and white ones when she got bored with it.

* Old dress patterns, bags of wool and knitting needles, buttons, ribbons and beads for when you're feeling creative.

Jumble sales

There is something nostalgic about a jumble sale – a great British institution that hung around long after the war ended. They are usually found in a church hall that smells of musty lavender and has a twenty pence entrance fee. The prices are wartime too. Five pence for a faux-fur stole will soon have you elbowing the grannies out of the way. You will leave with a warm glow, knowing you have contributed to the £35.24 and one peseta, which was raised for the Brownies' minibus trip to the lightship.

Vintage

Vintage is now the top end of the second-hand clothes market. Once a term used solely in wine and cheese circles, today it's one of fashion's favourite buzzwords. Modern high street clothes don't match up to vintage in the quality stakes, and don't have the satin linings, lined button holes and sheer attention to detail of older pieces.

Dita Von Teese and Scarlett Johansson have put old-school glamour back on the map. Chloë Sevigny and Winona Ryder are experts in vintage designer dressing, as are Keira Knightley and Reese Witherspoon. But don't think they have spent weeks trawling around their local flea markets and managed to find an old Azzaro dress hidden on the rails. They've simply sent their stylists round to LA's premier vintage clothing dealer, Decades (www.decadesinc.com). Cameron Silver does the trawling on their behalf, getting access to some of the dress collections of the rich and famous who call him when they are having a wardrobe clear-out. He specialises in 'pre-owned' clothing from designers, including Courrèges, Ossie Clark and Hermès.

Other landmark top-end vintage shops include Steinberg & Tolkien in London, a King's Road institution packed with everything from Edwardian ballgowns to a 1960s suit made from popcorn.

Virginia, in west London, has long been the ultimate vintage haunt, where everyone from John Galliano to Marc Jacobs has sent their scouts in search of a detail that could spawn an entire new collection. **Rellik**, in Portobello Road, is another favourite stomping ground, frequented by fashion's most influential tastemakers, like the stylist Venetia Scott, who consults for Marc Jacobs. One season, the hunt will be on for old school denim. Another, it will be vintage YSL. Occasionally a dress will simply be copied – it's amazing how, suddenly, an old classic can become the season's hottest look.

Trends come and go. And then they come again. And go just as quickly. How many times has the 1960s been revived in the past decade alone?

Happily, this means that you can keep ahead of the pack by shopping at vintage boutiques. Everything comes around in the end. It's simply a question of timing. Keep a look-out, too, for classic items that will never date. These are the pieces that fashion editors love – the trench coat, the white shirt, the pencil skirt, the cashmere twin set, the pea coat, the tuxedo, a great pair of jeans.

A few tips about buying vintage:
* old stains don't come out
* don't expect utter perfection (though you may get it!)
* vintage sizes are usually smaller so make sure you check all measurements

The stylist's best-kept secret

On the London scene, **Beyond Retro**, a vast warehouse of vintage clothing on Cheshire Street off Brick Lane, has become a fashion institution. Set up five years ago, way before the other retro shops, independent designers, and guerrilla art spaces made the area their home, it is a destination that only those in the know will ever find. There are no window displays, just industrial shutters and the promise of rows and rows of rails to riffle through; the 50,000 square foot warehouse stocks 10,000 garments, with 300 brought down to the shop floor daily.

Vintage addicts, including Dita Von Teese and Kelly Osborne, count Beyond Retro among their favourite places to shop. Designers use it for research. Robert Carey-Williams, who is based nearby, cut up the clothes to make his own designs for a recent show. The big denim and sports brands frequent the store searching for missing archive pieces. Pete Doherty practically lived there when he was in The Libertines. And when Pete became the ultimate icon of Dior menswear designer Hedi Slimane, the Beyond Retro look consequently filtered up to the highest echelons of Paris fashion.

Amber Butchart is Beyond Retro's onsite coordinator and trend analyst (yes, vintage shops really do have such people) and her job is to keep an eye on the catwalk trends, and on her savvy customers – fashion stylists and students – who often know what they want before the rest of us realise we want it too. Perennial bestsellers include prom dresses, interesting prints, hand-painted ties, and late 1970s and 1980s sports gear. This year's new bestseller is 1990s fluorescent colours.

Beyond Retro is not only a place to see and be seen in, everything you buy there has been recycled. Which means it's effortlessly ethical chic, and you might even get your hands on it before the design assistants of the big fashion houses. Not that this makes you feel smug or anything . . .

Just make sure you look the part when you go. You never know who you might be elbowing aside, as you work your way along the rails.

Recycled

This can mean one of two things: either the fabric that the garment is made from is waste (everything from old curtains to plastic bottles which can be used to make fleece), or pieces of unwanted clothes have been cut up and rehashed into something more desirable and up to date. Think Molly Ringwald in the brat pack film *Pretty in Pink*, only the 80s upside-down triangle she created was probably best left as the three dresses she started with.

Look twice, and it's clear that fashion is obsessed with recycling. Designers recycle ideas constantly. Whether it's looking through their own archives in search of a sleeve, a cuff, or a theme to inspire something new or scouring second-hand markets and vintage stores – buying up all the best items and putting prices at a premium (slightly annoying for the rest of us) – they're all at it.

The secret to getting a unique 'recycled' look is finding experts who know what trends work, and how to get the most out of unwanted garments. Sari Couture is Sital Haria and Sam Cook's label devoted to making clothes and accessories out of saris. Check out Junky Styling's wardrobe surgery, Goodone, who make great T-shirts and sporty one-offs from carefully chosen recycled fabrics, and Traid Remade – all feature later in these pages. You can even buy (or make your own) handmade shoes and bags made from waste materials (as you'll discover in chapter 9).

The best recycled clothes should never look as though they have been recycled. Instead, they should look beautifully made – using the best raw materials to start with. That's the idea behind From Somewhere at least. The label has recently opened its first boutique in west London, selling its simple, elegant clothes made from the off-cuts from some of the best textile mills in Italy. This is recycling at its most luxurious (see page 82 for more).

Names to remember

Junky Styling
Goodone
Traid
From Somewhere
Sari Couture

Online

A good place to start your ethical wardrobe is online. For a one-stop shop, try specialist websites like www.adili.com and www.thenatural store.co.uk. For everyday clothes www.peopletree.com is a great starting point. Browse the stocks of some of the smaller, independent boutiques, currently scouring the market for fashionable product. I'm thinking, in particular, of www.equaclothing.com, which already has its own celebrity fan base, and where you can shop without making any compromise on style.

For an exhaustive online shopping list, go to the Little Green Book at the back – you'll find everything you need . . .

The Beauty of Slow Fashion

Looking hot in haute couture

It could be argued that haute couture – the highest, most elite form of fashion, where exquisite dresses are made completely by hand, and fitted to the wearer like a second skin – is the most ethical fashion of all.

This is slow fashion at its most luxurious. The polar opposite of the throwaway stuff on the high street, money is no object for the buyers, so the amount of time spent on a single garment becomes utterly irrelevant. An evening dress might take several weeks, or months, to make from start to finish. Truly, it will take as long as it takes – as long as it is ready in time for the shows, which happen twice a year.

I have been into the ateliers of some of the famous French houses, like Yves Saint Laurent (when the designer himself was still in residence), and the embroidery houses like Lesage, which creates elaborate bead work, sequins and other lavish embellishments. I've watched suits being tailored, hems being stitched, seams and darts being pressed, and cloth being cut. The most skilled workers are treated with the greatest respect. And the more lowly seamstresses and other *petites mains* (as they are called) all operate in the sort of conditions that the average Bangladeshi seamstress could only dream of. The workers are highly unionised – and will strike at the drop of a thimble.

Of course, the use of fur and rare animal skins, and the ethics of spending upwards of £20,000 on a single frock that you will only wear once, are questionable. But there is something marvellously anachronistic about ordering clothes that will be made specifically to your measurements, and sewn by hand to the highest possible levels of perfection. On a less grandiose level, it is the equivalent of employing a seamstress to make your clothes (something my grandmother's generation did quite frequently) or making them yourself – though depending on your dressmaking skills, the result may be less than perfect.

These are clothes that will never end up in a landfill pit (though, occasionally, they do crop up in some of the well-heeled thrift shops on Manhattan's Upper West Side). These are clothes that have been made with so much care and consideration that they become precious objects. If we all had to wait for our clothes to be made, and treated the process with kid gloves and a bit more respect, perhaps our wardrobes would not be so crammed full of clothes we don't need and – half the time – don't even want.

That said, some of the society ladies and princesses who can afford to buy haute couture still love to shop at Gap and they don't just have floor-to-ceiling wardrobes, they have walk-in dressing rooms crammed with the stuff . . .

How to join a waiting list

If we want sustainable fashion that is fair to the maker, we are going to have to temper our habits. Quick, cheap fixes are not the answer, tempting though they may be. So, why not celebrate this fact by joining a waiting list?

Fashion companies love waiting lists. Sometimes, a much-publicised list for a particular shoe or bag is all part of the marketing spin to hype up a particular item or accessory. One season, it will be a Prada shoe. Another, it will be a Balenciaga bag. But the best waiting lists are for those pieces that really do take a long time and a particular set of skills to make. Some things simply cannot be rushed. To join a waiting list, you have to know exactly what you want, and be sure that you will still want it in a month or so's time when it arrives in store. It might be something you have seen on style.com the day after a show and if it's the piece of clothing you've been dreaming of all your life, then you should simply take the look number into the shop – these things are best done in person – and lay your claim to it.

Key items to look out for

The Hermès Birkin bag

Hermès are so discreet they don't like to talk about such vulgar things as waiting lists. But the French luxury goods company simply cannot keep up with demand for the bag it designed for Jane Birkin in 1984. Prices start at £2250 but if you want one you may have to wait depending on your choice of leather. This surely, is the ultimate in slow fashion. Each bag is handmade in the ateliers in Paris, taking up to twenty-five hours to be cut, stitched and finished. It might take you a lifetime to save up for one, and even then you will have to wait your turn. The thing about a Hermès bag is that it will last forever – it's the Land Rover of the bag world. Occasionally they come up for sale at auction houses like Christies. In 2007, a cherry red crocodile Birkin bag sold at auction there for an astounding (and world record-breaking) £36,000.

Azzedine Alaïa

The cult designer is a perfectionist who works outside of the traditional fashion seasons, refusing to create a new collection season after season. He shows his collections when he is ready, and not before. He also operates a very democratic business. At lunchtime, the entire team sits down for lunch together in the big kitchen at the atelier (where Alaïa also lives), like one big happy and unruly family. The prices however – around £1500 for a skirt – might leave you feeling a little breathless, but rest assured, these are clothes that women who can afford them keep and wear forever.

Alber Elbaz's designs for Lanvin

One of fashion's most self-effacing and humble designers is also one of its most influential. Since taking over at Lanvin, Alber Elbaz has made the label one of the most talked about and lusted after of our generation. His clothes have a vintage look about them, almost as though they have come from another time and place, but without ever looking retro. Any of his dresses will do. Guaranteed to become the heirlooms of the future, and clothes as beautiful as this never go out of date.

Roland Mouret

Hysteria surrounds this designer, and rightly so. His famous Galaxy dress was seriously worth waiting for (though you may have to leave it for a few years before you can get it out again). His collection for Gap had people adding their names to lists before they had even seen the clothes. His latest RM collection on sale November 2007, was available to pre-order on net-a-porter.com the day after he showed it during the Paris Haute Couture in July. At least you could never accuse Mr Mouret of waste; what he makes, he sells.

Bespoke suits are traditionally male territory, but that doesn't mean Savile Row is out of bounds for girls. Many tailors will make to measure for us too. Timothy Everest, who actually works near Spitalfields in London's East End, makes suits for Daniel Craig, Colin Firth and the England Football team, so you never know who you might meet when you turn up for a fitting. But be warned. If you are used to instant gratification, this really is a slow burn. Allow for a couple of months before your important meeting. Here's how it works.

How to order a bespoke suit
By Timothy Everest

1. *First impressions count.* The first meeting is a very important moment, because to make a good suit a good tailor has to understand exactly what the client needs. At this stage you have to talk to the tailor. Explain exactly what you want. A good tailor will listen carefully to find out what sort of person you are, what you like, why you want a bespoke suit and what you will use it for. You will discuss shape, fabric and style. The magic of the bespoke world starts from the precious relation between tailor and client.

2. *Measure up.* For a bespoke suit, we usually take twenty-five measurements. Just to give you an idea, for MTM suits (semi-bespoke, so half machine-made, half handmade) we take nine measurements. A bespoke suit is something unique, so it has to fit like a glove. For this to be possible you need the most precise idea of your client's body shape. A tailored suit can work wonders, correcting posture, emphasising your waist, or detracting attention from an area you are not so fond of.

3. *Choose a fabric.* There are millions of different types of fabric, and many different companies producing them. To choose the right fabric you have to understand what the client will use the suit for (special occasion, wedding or everyday suit). That's a good starting point. Then there are different weights

depending on the season and price, and obviously personal taste influences the choice a lot as well.

4. *Wait.* From the first fitting/meeting with the client to the second one, it takes something like four weeks. The client will try on a basted garment (with hand stitches and no linings) to make sure the production is going well.

5. *Patience!* There will usually be three fittings. It can be more, especially for a new client, or fewer if it's a regular client.

6. *Suits you madam!* The whole process from initial consultation to final suit will take eight to nine weeks. It will be well worth the wait – a suit made to fit your every curve.

For more information, or if you are in a hurry to start the long, slow process, go to www.timothyeverest.co.uk.

How to Get the Most out of Your Wardrobe

The secret to revitalising your look in the first place is to get organised. For an instant hit, without spending a penny, take a peek in your own wardrobe: go on, go right to the back. I bet you have all sorts of clothes in there that you haven't worn for years. You've probably forgotten you ever had them.

* Give your wardrobe an airing, swap the things you wear most frequently for the ones you've forgotten about, and wait for the compliments.

* Face up to the fact that there are items you are never, ever going to wear again.

* If you find clothes that you really don't want, but that you think someone else you know might like, organise a clothes swapping – or swishing – party (see page 139). It is important to invite friends who you know might like your cast-offs but also remember to invite friends whose style you admire. You never know what they might bring!

* Divide your cast-offs into separate piles for charity, swapping, customising, alterations and repairs.

* If you have good clothes that you would like to sell, you don't have to put them on eBay. There are some really good clothing exchanges that will give you a reasonable price for them.

* Old clothes that aren't good enough to sell can be given to your favourite charity (although we are getting rid of so many clothes now that some charity chops are getting very picky).

* Alternatively, put your discarded items into bags and post them in a textile recycling bin like Traid's.

* And if you want some fun (and a lovely warm feeling inside), it's worth joining your local freecycle community (see www.freecycle.org and www.whatismineisyours.com). You never know what your neighbours might like, or what they might give away.

Closet queens

If you need a working wardrobe sorting out fast, Anya Hindmarch recommends Shona Mac (www.shona mac.com), who provides a full range of services including wardrobe weeding. Shona Mac will sell items for you (in fact the website's a good place to buy too – a kind of ultra chic, edited-down version of eBay). Sometimes it helps to have someone go through your closet with you – they will be so much more ruthless than you are on your own. Women spend 85 per cent of their time wearing 15 per cent of their clothes, says Shona. Don't we know it? Instead, maximise the potential of what you've got – and perhaps generate some cash (and space on the rails) to buy a few more choice items.

Kira Jolliffe, who co-founded the fashion fanzine *Cheap Date*, also offers her advice and an injection of style as 'wardrobe sorter' (www.wardrobe woman.co.uk). Let Kira loose in your wardrobe for just three to four hours, and she promises to leave you feeling like a celebrity with a fabulous new wardrobe, without buying a single new item.

Spend a day doing repairs

Now you've cut down on your shopping, you can use your time more constructively. Zen slacker, Robert Twigger, suggested taking an entire day to sew on buttons and mend clothes in *The Idler's How to Save the World Without Really Trying*.

Instead of dashing around your local high street, shopping like a maniac, simply make yourself a nice big pot of tea (you can move on to cocktails after lunch), and get your sewing box out. You could even invite some friends round and make it a social occasion. Before you know it, you will have found yourself a craft circle. One thing is for sure, your wardrobe will thank you for it. I can get on with those trouser hems now, and I must fix the hem of my coat, and there are loads of buttons on their last thread . . .

How to sew on a button

* Choose a suitable button. Most companies provide spare ones – and sometimes a matching length of thread – with your garments. Always keep buttons that fall off, even if you don't sew them on straightaway. Everybody should have a button jar.
* Thread a needle with a double length of thread – not too long or you will end up with your knickers in a twist – and tie a knot at the end.
* Start underneath the button and make a small stitch to secure the knot. Poke the needle through one of the holes in the button. If the other buttons are sewn with a criss-cross effect, then do the same. If it's a parallel stitch, then copy that. Make several stitches to ensure it is strong.
* When you are finished, bring the needle to the back of the button and wrap the thread around the stitches several times to add strength.
* Poke the needle to the back of the garment again. Make a tight

double stitch to hold it all in place, and cut the thread close to the stitch. Easy!

Big ideas for your smalls

If your underwear drawer is anything like mine, it's a confused, pretty mess of polyester, elastane, cotton and nylon – and the odd flash of silk. The thing about underwear is that you can't recycle it – don't even go there! Charity shops don't want your greying bras and holey pants, and all that knicker elastic is going to take forever to biodegrade. So, here's what you *can* do:

* It's worth remembering that old cotton undies and T-shirts can enjoy a second life: they make great dusters!
* Alternatively, the American site SuperNaturale is taking recycling to the next level . . . it features an ingenious way to use your old T-shirt – with a few stitches you can turn them into a brand new pair of pants. Now this may be a little Maria Von Trapp for me, but if you fancy a go, download the pattern off their site: www.supernaturale.com
* Finally, Patagonia is the first company to take back other clothing brands – from longjohns to fleeces and organic T-shirts. They'll recycle and transform your cast-offs into new shell jackets, bras, knickers and even sweet strappy dresses.

Putting the fashion in eco fashion
By Sarah Ratty, designer

Eco fashion has changed a lot since I started my Conscious Earthwear Label in 1992. Then, it was very crusty – super crusty! I started making beautiful anarchic creations that were, well, I don't know what we were thinking of, or who the hell we thought was going to wear them – they were bonkers!

The recycled Aran dress I did was startling. But we wore them; it was about being free and having fun with it and having no restrictions. I'd think, 'I'm going to make something out of all this waste.' I remember going to Oxfam Waste Savers and asking 'What do you get loads of?' And they said Aran sweaters. So I thought, 'Let's do something with them then,' and that's what we did. I got them all laundered and I just cut them apart and draped them on the stand and saw what they could do and made these wild things. I loved it because if I wanted a pocket I'd just take a pocket and put it on there and that was really exciting. I enjoyed doing that. It was really good fun. I'd done a bit of voluntary work for Oxfam and I knew how it all worked. I just asked them to save me certain colours and they did and that's how it all happened.

In those days, I had a studio in Iliffe Yard in south London, and we would bring back all the Aran sweaters from being laundered, and cut them all up. I remember we got loads of outworkers on an estate in Peckham, and we'd be running round with all these shopping trolleys full of sweaters. Quite hilarious really! It got to a point where I couldn't cope with the demand. It was such a hard slog; it was like working with one hand tied behind your back; so labour intensive that I started to question if it really was environmental after all!

Then we had a breakthrough and began to find fabrics, on the roll, that were made out of recycled polymer from old soda bottles, and other fabrics that were environmentally produced. That made my life a bit easier. While it was fun doing the craft side of things, it's quite nice to be able to cut into a roll of cloth and make something in a more conventional way.

I have a fashion background and good design has always been at the forefront of what I do. My mother taught fashion at Brighton Art College, where she worked with Barbara Hulanicki who went on to found Biba, and she taught me fashion from the age of four. I like to create beauty in the world and make everyone happier, and I believe fashion has a really great role to play there. OK, it can be vacuous, but equally, I think if you put something on that makes you feel good, that affects everything you do. It makes you feel more confident as a person and that's got to be important.

I'm on the textile advisory committee for the Soil Association. It's about what fibres and what chemicals are permissible for organic fabrics, what dyes they can use and what processes they can use. I look at it from a designer's viewpoint so I help them to interpret those principles for the real world. I've managed to get them to accept a 10 per cent trim that isn't necessarily organic. As a designer, this makes a huge difference to the collections. You need to embellish things and make them exciting.

Now you can get organic cotton in fabrics that feel lovely. There are so many exciting things – hemp silk is beautiful, it holds the light and feels very glamorous. We've got a bamboo denim, which is so soft, and bamboo jersey-knit lingerie and soft separates that feel like silk.

I haven't given clothes to celebrities, but some of them – including Cate Blanchett – buy my designs, which is great. I am really excited about the way the whole industry is now taking green fashion seriously and how it is prompting change in such positive ways. Ethical fashion is not something that we should aspire towards by 2012. It's something to get on with and do today! I want to show people that it's easy, it can happen, and it is right here, right now, every day. I feel quite passionately about that. It's great to see that a movement I was part of in the early 1990s is growing so quickly and that eco fashion has proved that it is not a passing trend. It's here now and it's the future too.

FAIRTRADE

2

I Shop, therefore I Am Ethical

I Shop, therefore I Am Ethical

'Fashion your life as a garland of beautiful deeds'

Buddha

The Fashionista's Dilemma

We love clothes. We love to shop. Some of us would say we live to shop. And if you're smart, this can be a good thing. The trick is to direct your spending power. As more businesses realise that they can produce clothes in an ethical, environmentally sympathetic way *and* make money in the process, you will find that there are more and more ways to spend your money. This chapter is all about proving that you can shop and still be a responsible, caring, sharing member of the human race. Hurrah!

A hard day's shop

There's nothing like coming home after a hard day's shopping, laden with bags. You've got lots of them – filled with the shoes you've been pining for, some hot dresses, trousers for work, underwear – because you can never have enough (even though you can hardly close your knicker drawer these days), and armfuls and armfuls of sparkly accessories. You can't wait to unwrap and try them on. You've splashed out on a couple of expensive pieces, but you've got some bargains too. At the back of your mind, you are conscious that perhaps seven carrier bags was slightly overdoing it. But three of them are paper, at least. And you are

feeling a happy glow of satisfaction. You know what they say –
retail is one of the best forms of therapy.

Unfortunately, for the conscientious fashionista, it won't be long
before the glow fades, and the guilt sets in. Guilt and shopping go
hand in hand for most of us these days. It's not just that you are
spending beyond your means and are on your second interest-free
credit card transfer. The minute you start to consider who has made
your clothes, in what sort of conditions, and how little they are being
paid, impulse shopping can start to feel rather uncomfortable.

Safia Minney founded People Tree, the Fair
Trade clothing company, to try to redress the
balance and to empower people who make her
clothes so that they are not being exploited, harassed
or underpaid in their workplace. She also tries to create
work opportunities in rural areas so that villagers are not forced to
move to the overcrowded cities to find employment. She is
passionate about workers' rights and you can catch a glimpse of
her life later in the chapter when you read her postcard from
Bangladesh.

And then there are issues about ecology. Synthetic fibres might
be miraculous in that they don't need to be ironed and are
incredibly hardwearing, but they are carbon intensive. The fashion
industry pumps out carbon dioxide like it is, well, going out of
fashion. And natural fibres aren't much better. Pesticides used to
grow cotton are harmful to the eco structure, as well as to the
farmers who grow them.

Katharine Hamnett has been campaigning for organic farming
methods in cotton since the late 1980s, and has recently seen years
of hard work begin to come to fruition with her Katharine E
Hamnett line, and her collection of organic cotton basics for Tesco.
She explains why organic cotton is so important – and gives you a
few pointers on page 40 of what you can do to help her change the
industry.

The problem is, once you start to consider all of these issues, there is no turning back. Which is why ethical fashion is so much more than a passing fad. Just as, once you've made the decision to buy organic carrots, it seems pointless then to buy non-organic broccoli and apples, so too, once you've bought an item of clothing made from organic cotton, you seriously question yourself when you buy something made from cotton farmed using toxic chemicals.

To help you balance your shopping pleasure and those inevitable ethical and social dilemmas, here are some points to consider before you buy:

Ask yourself

* Do I really need it?
* Why is it so cheap?
* What is it made of?
* Is the cotton organic?
* Is it fair trade?
* Has it been made in China, where unions are illegal?
* Has it been made in a sweatshop, possibly using child labour?
* How much do you think the people making it were paid?
* How many air miles, and how many carbon emissions has this single garment produced?
* Is the packaging excessive?
* Has it been recycled?
* Can it be recycled?
* Will it add to the 500,000 tonnes of unwanted clothing that ends up as landfill each year in the UK alone?
* Is that fur trim real?
* Can it be washed, or is it dry clean only?

All this and you haven't even got as far as the fitting room! Never mind 'Does my bum look big in this?' Or even, 'What's the credit card bill going to look like?' We ethical girls have weightier matters to consider!

What's wrong with cotton?
By Katharine Hamnett

" The fashion industry is one of the largest in the industrialised economy. It employs a billion people, uses a whopping 25 per cent of the world's pesticides, and causes devastating poverty across the developing world.

Twenty thousand people die each year from pesticide poisoning in cotton agriculture. And then there is the massive waste of water, and the criminal CO_2 emissions. The business is profligate and it impacts on every possible level.

How much longer is this going to go on for? There are companies who are quite happy to make their money paying people five cents an hour and then spending the enormous profits on repulsively vulgar six-floor yachts with helicopters and rowing boats. The lack of conscience is staggering!

In the old days, I'd go to Italian fabric fairs desperately looking for organic cotton with very few leads. You'd go on stands and they'd say, 'Why should we do it because you are the only one asking for it?' It made me so angry with the industry.

When I went to Mali with Oxfam in 1993, I saw at first hand the devastating poverty of cotton farmers in a country where cotton is the second largest export after gold. I met a cotton farmer's wife who, because of her own meagre diet, had lost two children at the breast from malnutrition. Her fate is typical of cotton-farming families across Africa.

With organic cotton, farmers get a 50 per cent increase in their income. The more organic cotton we consume the clearer the message to the brokers that we need farmers to grow organic.

A farmer has to be pesticide free for three years before he can be organic and we have talked to the Soil Association about developing another layer of certification because it is very difficult for farmers to convert (because in the conversion period they may get a drop in yield).

You've really got to know your facts. In the beginning, when we started campaigning for organic in the late 1980s, newspapers like the *Guardian* said that organic cotton was brown and lumpy. Where did they get that from?! Go into the V&A and look at any pre-1880 clothing and you'll find finer fabrics than anything being produced today. The cotton is actually more delicate to the touch – it's softer, more beautiful, sophisticated, and that's as it should be. Our stuff is actually nice. You should try it!

Katharine Hamnett's tips for effecting change

* By insisting on organic cotton and fair pay for garment workers, and by paying 1 per cent more for a T-shirt, you can change the world and make it a better and safer place.
* Write to the producers of your favourite brands. Tell them that you love their brand but only want to buy cotton from them if it is organic. Ask what organic stock they carry and inform them that if they don't have any you are going to stop buying their brand until they can supply organic products. Tell your friends to do the same.
* When you go into large stores ask them if they have any products in organic cotton. Tell them that it is the only cotton you are going to buy.
* Buy at least one organic cotton garment every season. Also look out for organic cotton towels and sheets.
* Support the Environmental Justice Foundation's Cotton Campaign (and buy a T-shirt). Show your friends and family the EJF's film *White Gold – the True Cost of Cotton*, about the shocking human rights and environmental abuses occurring in Uzbekistan. You can download the film for free at www.ejfoundation.org/cotton.
* For a list of all the wonderful places to find the best organic and

Fair trade cotton ranges on the high street go to the Little Green Book shopping directory.

How to Shop without Guilt

Just to prove that you don't have to shop in funny little hippy shops that sell sunflower seeds and hemp shirts, it's worth a quick trip down Oxford Street – Mecca for shopaholics the world over – to show you how you can shop with a conscience.

First stop, Topshop. Forget the Kate Moss mini-me range and go straight for the People Tree for Topshop collection, which is made using organic cotton grown in Mali and Cameroon. Get your accessories from Made (more on this on page 236), and check out Hug, Gossypium and Kuyichi jeans – all great clothes, so no hardship there.

Next, it's on to Urban Outfitters for your Ethical Justice Foundation T-shirt. Look out for Katharine Hamnett's classic 'Save the Future' vest.

Then, call into H&M and indulge in their organic cotton range. This has been a hit since arriving in the shops in spring 2007 and looks set to expand. The more you support it and choose organic over the other cotton clothes they sell, the bigger and more interesting the collection will become. If you want to ensure that the workers who make the clothes are doing so in decent conditions, and with fair pay, write to your local store (see the Little Green Book at the back for a letter template).

Though Gap has had its share of bad press in the past, it is responding to customer demand in a big way. Its (Product) Red basics support trade in Africa and 50 per cent of the profits goes towards fighting AIDS.

If you have a problem with big corporations, remember that

they are the ones with the power, and if they change, it creates big waves that really make a difference. Even if it is all a big PR promotion, what does it matter? They are doing something. And if you show your support, they will do more.

Bored with the crowds on Oxford Street? Take a detour down Carnaby Street, and you can continue your guilt-free spree as you shop in Timberland and American Apparel. Make sure you ask for their organic collection and if they don't have it, tell them you want it. Nip round the corner to Neal's Yard Remedies, and then finish off with a splurge in Liberty's beauty department, where you can pamper yourself with Aveda, Ren, Korres and other natural and organic ranges. As a consumer, you have fantastic power. Don't forget to use it!

High Street Heroes

As Katharine Hamnett has proved, the high street has the power to lead the way, responding to the needs and demands of the ethical consumer. For your convenience, here are some of the best.

American Apparel

Sweatshop-free T-shirts. Now there's a thing. American Apparel has all sorts of perks for the workers at its LA factory, including free yoga and overtime pay. They also do a small line in organic cotton.

Gant

Gant is a secret ethical hero. The company's credo is 'blue is the new green' (catchy!) and a percentage of its profits goes to saving our oceans.

✿ *Marks & Spencer*

Leading the march towards a cleaner, fairer shopping experience, M&S have unveiled Plan A, a £200 million scheme to become carbon neutral by 2012 – a commitment that would be the equivalent of taking 100,000 cars off the road. The company also aims to stop sending waste to landfill sites by that date, increase the amount of food sourced locally and regionally and increase the use of recycled materials. M&S already uses one-third of the world's Fairtrade cotton and by 2012 they are aiming to ensure that 5 per cent of their cotton is organic.

✿ *Nike*

Nike has committed to eliminating 'excessive overtime in contract factories' and is already using 5 per cent organic cotton in all of its cotton product, as well as expanding its 100 per cent organic ranges. Log on to www.nike.com and you can read the company's CSR report, complete with info on how it is attempting to reduce its carbon footprint of 1.36 million metric tonnes. Good news on the green front too: you can recycle your trainers at Nike stores (see page 227). Keep the pressure up and the company will go further.

✿ *Sainsbury's*

The biggest retailer of fair trade products in the UK, Sainsbury's new Tu range of basic clothing is made using Fairtrade cotton from West Africa and its shoppers are made from sustainable jute. The company partnered with We Are What We Do to sell the Anya Hindmarch 'I'm Not a Plastic Bag' shopper. More on this later . . .

Tesco

A surprise entry perhaps, but Tesco deserves a mention for working with Katharine Hamnett for her Choose Love organic cotton collection. Tesco agreed to Hamnett's strict rules of compliance, not just on the organic cotton provision (350 tonnes of it from a mill in India) but in terms of labour regulations. Let's hope it filters through into all areas of their clothing manufacture.

 *Timberland*

Timberland makes every effort to be sustainable. Their shoeboxes come with 'nutrition labels', where you can see at a glance the energy each pair of shoes has taken to produce, how much of that energy is renewable, and the percentage of factories assessed against their code of conduct.

 Topshop

Topshop's collaboration with everyone's favourite Fair Trade clothing company, People Tree, has been a huge success, as has it's Made 'Trade not aid' jewellery concession. Other projects include serious investment in Fairtrade cotton at the seed stage to help coordinate a project with the Global Mamas. Kate Moss, take note!

● ★ ● ★

A Postcard from Bangladesh

Dear Green is the New Black

I am writing this from my favourite village in the world. Thonapara Swallows is in northern Bangladesh. In the early morning the village smells of clay as the dew lifts from the dirt paths between mud houses, and the villagers brush their teeth with twigs they've chewed to form bristles. As the women sweep around their homes and feed their children breakfast before school, others start their work. There are cottage industries everywhere: one uses a small sugarcane-crushing machine and another boils it to make sugar. Others are rearing chickens and goats, others tending the vegetable gardens that grow on the roofs of their simple homes. The men are working in the fields and fishing.

Romantic as village life looks, it can become a struggle. International agricultural subsidies and market liberalisation undermine local village economies, and machines have nearly wiped out their livelihoods. Wasn't it enough that the British cut off the fingers of the world-famous Muslim weavers over one hundred years ago to secure markets for Lancashire mills?

Fair trade and development assistance have helped local initiatives to take root and flourish in villages like Swallows. There's now a school for 320 poor children, a handicraft project that provides employment for 150 people, and a programme of social support for the wider community. Women have been trained, and developed their skills so that they can make products that will not look out of place in the best fashion stores in London and Tokyo. In typical Ghandian tradition they use bobbin thread, hand-weave fabric, then hand-embroider and embellish clothing, as well as tailoring it. There is also a day-care centre for the women's babies and pre-school children. Fair trade fashion has helped them double their earnings so they can now earn a wage in excess of that of a garment factory worker in Dhaka, and staff live as families in the village where living costs are a third of the capital.

People Tree is planning to grow organic cotton near Swallows too – to provide a cash crop for the landless farmers' community in the 'Char' land. I was shocked that many of the four- to twelve-year-olds there couldn't afford to take the boat across the river to attend school. We plan to send a teacher to them, to help the farmers' children get the chance of an education.

This is the reality half our world faces – no opportunities for a livelihood that meets their basic needs and an economic policy that undermines their very existence. That is why ethical fashion – meeting basic standards of Social Compliance for garment factories' workers – is the least the British high street should do.

Factory fires and collapses have claimed the lives of hundreds in the last two years in Bangladesh alone and average earnings do not allow the women to feed themselves adequately. In India, conventional cotton claims the lives of hundreds of farmers. As the Hindu newspaper reported last year, pesticides are no longer able to control pests: 'Cotton farmers are in the forefront of those committing suicide. Their costs have way outstripped their incomes.'

The goal should not be ethical fashion but fair trade fashion – supporting the most marginalized farmers and artisans to enjoy the benefits of the rag trade, and developing strong, thriving and sustainable local communities.

Love, Safia Minney
Founder of the Fair Trade fashion company – People Tree

How Not to Shop

On the whole, joining a queue or taking part in any form of mass hysteria on the high street is to be avoided. It doesn't matter whether it's for Kate Moss, Stella McCartney, or even Anya Hindmarch – ethical style and scrums just don't mix.

In April 2007, when Primark opened its flagship store in central London, mounted police were needed to control the sort of crowds normally encountered at football matches. Quite apart from the fact that trampling other shoppers underfoot is plain rude, if you can afford to buy a cheap, cashmere jumper in every colour, then you can afford to make a much stronger fashion statement. Buy just one, stand-out, fashion-conscious top, that has been made without the exploitation of every resource and human hand along the way, and you will have guaranteed style (and moral) superiority.

If it's discount clothes that you're after, TK Maxx is your best bet (or Century 21 if you are in New York). At TK Maxx, you are getting the ends of lines that haven't otherwise sold. Which means you can feel justified shopping to your heart's content, responsibly mopping up the fashion world's surplus.

Go local

The smart way to cut down on your carbon footprint is to shop local, and shop small. Shopping malls are overheated, overlit and increasingly overcrowded. Worst of all, they are speeding the end of individual chic, as independent shops and boutiques are edged out, unable to compete with the high rents. OK, so you are protected from the wind and the rain indoors, but one too many escalators and a few too many plastic palm trees and you might start feeling a little queasy.

Opt instead for a street market or – if you are lucky enough to still have one – your local village or town centre. Take the bus, cycle (see page 187 on how to do so in style) or walk. In 2006

Friends of the Earth launched its Shop Local First campaign, urging shoppers to support local businesses instead of driving to the nearest supermarket. More than 2000 independent shops went out of business in the UK in 2004. As more and more Starbucks move into your high street (there are now over 3000 branded coffee outlets in the UK, opening at a rate of nearly one a day), fewer independent shops, not to mention lovely, old-fashioned tea rooms, will be able to compete.

Don't you hate it when you visit a different town and it feels identical to the one you just left? Our high streets are beginning to feel as though they have come straight from Legoland. And the sad thing is, this isn't something that's just happened. It's down to all of us. As consumers, we are the ones with the power to shape our own world. And if we spent the £1.3 billion we spend on branded coffee each year at our local sandwich shop or deli – or better yet, local button shop (who still has one of those?!) – perhaps the streets would start to look a little less bland.

Shopping malls are, of course, designed around the car and are often impossible to get to unless you can drive. A far better excuse for those CO_2 emissions, however, is getting to and from car boot sales.

●★●★

Driving pleasure

Getting up with the larks and setting off with a car full of unwanted junk for a hard day's booting is one of life's great pleasures (once you've got over the shock of having to drag yourself out of bed so early). Go with a friend or loved one, pack a flask of coffee and some sandwiches (bagels filled with smoked mackerel, mayonnaise and black pepper are my favourite). You'll need to ram your car as full of stuff as you possibly can, and will inevitably find yourself wandering around your home at the last minute, taking books off shelves, packing up your old china, and getting rid of unworn, unwanted shoes.

It's fun to see punters haggling over spending 50p on your once-treasured belongings, and there's a real community spirit about car boot sales.

Get to know the people selling around you, and you develop a keen sense of who is buying to re-sell on eBay (hike up your prices); students out for a bargain (round down the price); and people who genuinely have no money (give it to them for free).

There is nothing quite like the sense of satisfaction when you set off back home. You've had a clear-out, your stuff has gone to a good home, and you've made some money in the process!

If you are a buyer rather than a seller, you really do feel pleased with yourself if you can drag yourself out of bed early and get some extra shopping in while everyone else is sleeping. The prices at boot sales are so low you may feel bad paying 20p for some Linda Farrow-esque sunnies. Resist the temptation to push the price up!

To find your nearest boot sale – whether you want to sell or buy – look out for posters on your local school playing fields or go to www.carbootjunction.com or www.gumtree.com for listings.

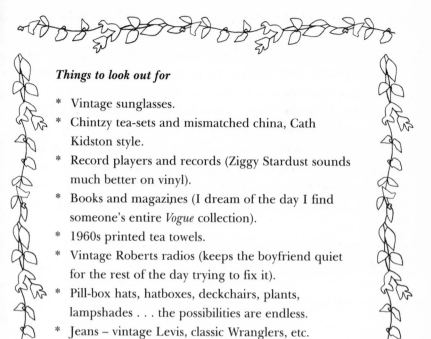

Things to look out for

* Vintage sunglasses.
* Chintzy tea-sets and mismatched china, Cath Kidston style.
* Record players and records (Ziggy Stardust sounds much better on vinyl).
* Books and magazines (I dream of the day I find someone's entire *Vogue* collection).
* 1960s printed tea towels.
* Vintage Roberts radios (keeps the boyfriend quiet for the rest of the day trying to fix it).
* Pill-box hats, hatboxes, deckchairs, plants, lampshades . . . the possibilities are endless.
* Jeans – vintage Levis, classic Wranglers, etc.
* Children's clothes – often unworn!

Baby Steps

For many of us, a greener lifestyle starts with babies. If you see yourself as a bit of a lost cause (in which case, don't be so pessimistic – there's still tonnes you can do!) you can at least start off the next generation in all the right ways. A lot of the women I talked to for this book said that the defining moment for them turning organic was when they started a family. Somehow babies give us a heightened sensibility. Not only do we want to feed them purely organic baby rice, we also want them to feel unbleached, organic cotton next to their skin. Chemicals and babies simply don't mix. And, thankfully, the really young are superbly catered for with all things organic – from their first mouthfuls of food to their babygros and even their nappies. The baby universe is organic-tastic, which is just as it should be. And as babies grow into toddlers, they might even progress on to a bit of hemp, or silky bamboo, courtesy of the yoga-loving, hippy-dippy, Kent farm-based company Tatty Bumpkin.

There are endless ranges to choose from, whether you go for Green Baby or Marks & Spencer's Fairtrade and organic cotton baby basics. And it's a great way of buying ethical by proxy. Somehow you can justify spending a bit extra when it's for your offspring.

Green babies
By Sheherazade Goldsmith

My husband might be the editor of the *Ecologist*, but I'm not a die-hard environmentalist by any stretch of the imagination. Everything I've started to do, I've done because of my three kids. When you have kids, you begin to question everything. I want to make sure my children stay as healthy as I can possibly make them. I want to protect the countryside for them; I want them to always be able to experience the same landscapes, to enjoy nature, to go snorkelling and see beautiful reefs. When I see poverty in other countries involving children, I always think, how would I feel if that was my child?

I can't claim to have used washable nappies until my third child. I always used Tushies, which were new when Uma was born. I was aware of the gel debate, but Uma got potty trained really early, partly because the nappies were so big they made her walk funny, and it was the summer, so I just thought I would let her not wear nappies. By the time I got to the third baby though, I decided to try an alternative. I used washable nappies and they are truly so much easier than I thought.

A major concern was that the cot was made from untreated wood – I didn't want the baby pulling herself up and sucking on something that had been treated with chemicals. The mattress had to be organic cotton. Things have changed in the seven years since I had Uma. There's so much good organic baby stuff now, like Green Baby, which I see a lot on the high street. When Uma was born, the organic babygros were only available in oatmeal, but now there's tonnes of brightly coloured stuff everywhere. With organic cotton, it's about the amount of pesticides being used to spray the cotton. Fairt trade is really important – making sure the farmers aren't suffering at our – and our children's – expense. **99**

Growing up with natural style
By Pearl Lowe

66 I love to dress the children in vintage clothes. I put my baby Betty in Victorian dresses and old-fashioned smocks that I get off eBay and cute woolly tights. I put Frankie in Graham Coxon-style glasses that he loves and woolly tank tops. Everything is vintage – it's better quality. I used to do it to Daisy as well. I just loved her looking like 'a proper little girl'. She got fed up at seven though, and used to complain that she wanted to dress like a Spice Girl.

I love Daniel Galvin's junior Hairjuice range for the kids (see www.danielgalvin.com). It's organic, which is great for Frankie and the baby because they suffer from eczema. I am fanatical about their diet because of this; everything must be organic; they can't even have conventional tomato ketchup. **99**

Through the keyhole with Bay Garnett

We all have guilty secrets lurking at the back of our wardrobes. Even with the best of intentions, our clothes are a mix of the ethical and the unethical, the natural and the synthetic, the beautiful and the ugly, the new and the old . . . and we all have a few things that should probably never see the light of day again. Here, Bay Garnett, stylist and co-founder of *Cheap Date* magazine, lets us have a peek into her wardrobes – all four of them.

* At the moment I have about ten handbags.
* I never clear out my wardrobes any more, as I have finally minimised them down to the essential pieces that for many reasons, whether they are really personal pieces or have a history, I could not throw away. Everything I have now I will have forever. Particular favourites include a banana-print top from New York Cancer Care charity shop, which featured in a *Vogue* shoot with Kate Moss (afterwards a very similar version appeared on the Chloé catwalk and was copied all over the high street); a black-sequined top that I wore to a circus party, where I met my current boyfriend (the whole night was sparkly and

it was as if the top had caused that); and a big, ethnic belt, which also featured in a *Vogue* shoot.

* I mainly shop at thrift shops and designers. I love Louis Vuitton and Chanel. My favourite thrift shops are in New York, where I lived when I was editing *Cheap Date* – on the Upper East Side, 3rd Avenue – and in Queens or the Bronx.
* I buy my underwear and basics from M&S and would definitely consider their organic range if it was nice enough.
* I wear 10 to 20 per cent of my wardrobe. I'm a bit busy to bother with most of it, as I've just had a baby.
* I never really mend my clothes, unless it is something really special.
* The oldest item in my wardrobe is an original punk T-shirt from the early 1980s, black, with zips all over it.
* I am never tempted by fast fashion. Those clothes are horrible. I would rather get something second-hand for the same price.
* My guilty secret is that I wear fur – but never new, only very old vintage fox furs.

3

Occasion Wear

Occasion Wear

'Wearing the correct dress for any occasion is a matter of good manners'

Loretta Young

Your Capsule Wardrobe

Now you've cut down on the amount of clothes you are buying and rediscovered lost favourites, looking great should be a cinch. The fact that you have given your wardrobe more thought and a good shake-up will make it easier to navigate. Your clothes will be able to breathe – and so will you. And it will be much easier to get dressed in the morning, without simply wearing the same three things that happen to be at the top of the pile in rotation (which is what I used to do).

Looking great will still require planning, or course. For starters, there's the challenge of global warming.

The new seasons

As the earth heats up, and seasonal confusion becomes the norm, the fashion industry seems to be going into overdrive, making more and more collections to cover all bases. Traditionally, summer clothes go into the shops as soon as the January sales are over, and winter coats go on sale in the heat of August. This has always felt wrong – the fashion equivalent of buying strawberries out of season. Increasingly, the clothes on the rails do not seem to have anything to do with the realities of our weather: the fact that winter has got shorter and summer longer – and if anything, the seasons are all merging into one.

The response from high-end designers is to start making pre-collections and pre-pre-collections, as well as cruise collections, traditionally aimed at wealthy ladies who trip off on a cruise in November, in search of winter sun. Meanwhile, the high street is hedging its bets by simply producing a new collection every few weeks, hoping that if there's a random heat wave in April, there will be something to buy. And of course, the more clothes we produce, the more carbon emissions we create, the bigger the hole gets in the ozone, and the more skewed the seasons become. It's all one big unholy circle.

The secret for dressing appropriately for the new seasons is surely about layers, which is possibly why layering has been such a big trend for the past few seasons. The designers *are* responding to our needs after all. Marc Jacobs does care. These days, it's not about different types of clothing for winter and summer. It's simply about how many layers you are wearing, allowing you to adapt to the challenges of a steaming hot underground train on a December morning, or an April day that starts off frosty and ends with an afternoon of blazing sunshine.

In effect, we don't need to change our clothes between the seasons. We just need to be equipped for every seasonal eventuality, every day, making it even more important that the clothes we buy are timeless, seasonless and easy to put on or take off according to the increasingly volatile whims of the weather.

If you are serious about wardrobe efficiency, you should make a list of items you need, and buy them when you see them. Try not to be seduced by the constant turnover of goodies in the high street, where new collections seem to appear every few weeks. Instead, have a core of staple pieces that you wear frequently. And when buying staples, remember that the better the quality the longer it will last. It is worth using the price-per-wear calculator to justify the expense. A £12 top that will fall apart in the first wash suddenly doesn't seem such good value as a £60 top that will last for years and years.

To get you started (and to give us all something to aim towards), your basic capsule wardrobe would look something like this:

* **Organic jeans** – see page 65 to help you choose. Once you've made sure the denim is organic, you can concentrate on finding the perfect fit.
* **T-shirts** – look out for organic cotton or bamboo. Try Katharine Hamnett or, for something plain, Gossypium.
* **A good jacket** – you can splurge on this as you want something that will last season after season preferably.
* **A handful of dresses** (rather than my forty-one. Oops!) – go for Ciel, Enamore or, for a party dress, Debbi Little. If you are on the high street, check out H&M's organic cotton range or see what People Tree has to offer.
* **Trousers** – try Amana, Katharine E Hamnett, Stewart & Brown, Noir or Wildlife Works.
* **A skirt** – check out Stewart & Brown, People Tree, Howies, or Patagonia.
* **A coat or two** – varying in weights. Try buying vintage for a really good quality coat, either well tailored or a 1950s trapeze.
* **A raincoat** – again, a vintage (or new) Burberry or Aquascutum Mac will last a lifetime. Check your mother's wardrobe to see if she has one that she's forgotten about.
* **Tops** – shirts, tunics or blouses. Try Edun, Stewart & Brown or any of the high street's organic cotton ranges.
* **A cardigan** and a couple of jumpers for chilly days or for when you don't want to turn the thermostat up a degree or two. Karen Cole makes wonderful knitwear using New Zealand Merino wool, and the sheep she uses haven't undergone the cruel practice of mulesing, used to control flystrike: www.karencole.co.uk.

* **Underwear** – enough knickers and bras to get you through the week you don't put a wash on. Try M&S Fairtrade, Enamore; and Ciel.
* **Shoes** – enough shoes to make you happy, without creating your own miniature shoe mountain. Go to page 212 for inspiration here.
* **Finishing touches** – a sprinkling of accessories to brighten your days and nights. Make sure you check out Made, and keep your eyes peeled for a good second-hand belt or bag.

You'll also benefit from a few statement pieces – a really beautiful coat, or a particularly striking top – to keep things interesting. This isn't an exercise in deprivation. It's just about making the most of what you have without buying excessive amounts of clothes from one season (or week) to the next. Just try to remind yourself: less is better.

The secret is choosing special items that you won't get bored with. I have a plain black crepe dress by the Belgian designer Martin Margiela, which is my trusty LBD. It is one of his replica vintage pieces (he is the king of recycling), a copy of a 1980s batwing dress, and is elasticated in the middle. Its simplicity makes it timeless. The weight of the crepe makes it feel luxurious every time I put it on. I must confess, it was what we fashion writers like to call 'an investment buy' (that is, I couldn't afford it and only bought it because I was in Paris and it's easier to spend in another currency), but I know that I will never tire of it, even if my friends and colleagues do.

How to Be Sustainable and Sexy

Seductive smalls

The logical place to start building your ethical wardrobe is next to your skin. There is something seductive about knowing that your basics are made from the purest, most natural materials Mother Nature can provide. But try to find an everyday, ethical bra, and you'll soon realise how limited your options are. On the UK high street there's the odd organic underwear set at American Apparel, and some good smalls by Gossypium. And of course, M&S has a Fairtrade cotton vest or two. But really, it's thin pickings.

Bras seem to be all about high technology these days – and that means a good dose of synthetic materials that are almost impossible to recycle. I look through my collection of old M&S bras, and there's lots of see-through rubbery latex stuff on the inside to hold them in place and endless elastic, plastic and metal mixed in. I don't think there is a natural thread in one of them. I suspect that if I threw one in the compost heap, very little of it would decompose. While this is a great argument for not burning your bras (far too many nasty fumes!), there is still a lot of work to be done to find a biodegradable bra that lifts, divides, and plunges in all the right places.

I decide to order online and am excited when a package arrives in the post the next day from The Natural Store. Inside, delicately wrapped in tissue paper, is **Ciel**'s organic cotton Cache Coeur bra. I was so excited to have found such a pretty everyday bra that I clicked it into my shopping basket without even worrying about the £32 price tag. Now I wouldn't normally dream of ordering a bra online, given that you can't try it on first. But this isn't about fit. It's about finding a solution to two problems: a piece of underwear that has not polluted the planet, and something to replace my horribly grey M&S collection.

Ciel have gone for a simple crossover design, trimmed with machine-embroidered 'lace'. There aren't any wires in it. There aren't even any hooks and eyes. But I'm sure it will be very comfortable, if minimally supportive. Natural, I suppose, is the word I'm looking for. I should have ordered the matching knickers too. Nevertheless, I feel as though I have made a step towards a cleaner, fresher Planet Fashion.

With underwear, however, it's not just about support. There are times when we demand a little romance from our undies too. But is it truly possible to be both sustainable and sexy? Hemp might be strong; it might grow like a weed without the need for pesticides; it might make a good sturdy, rugged T-shirt. But is it sexy? And do I really need to advertise the fact that I love the planet on my knickers, no matter how pretty, or right on, they are?

The Brighton-based designers, **Enamore**, have managed to achieve the impossible. The fact that their luxurious underwear – lingerie in the old-fashioned sense of the world – is 60 per cent hemp is almost secondary. The other 40 per cent silk makes all the difference and the result is 100 per cent vamp. As always, design is of the essence and Enamore know how to make a pair of saucy knickers. The fact that they make use of sustainable resources is the cherry on top. And best of all, Enamore don't stop at knickers. They make fabulous bras too – with vintage lace and everything! It's all very 1940s pin-up – the sort of thing that would inspire Dita Von Teese to get her fan out. Now all you need is a few scented candles (Natural Magic candles are organic), some boudoir furnishings and a matching bamboo silk robe from Eco Boudoir, a little carefully chosen music and (so I'm told) some silky bamboo sheets, and see where the mood takes you.

Working girl: what the green goddess wears to the office

Corporate life and green living are not traditionally the easiest of companions. But there is no reason why they shouldn't be. Going green makes good business sense, and doing it in sustainable pinstripes is guaranteed to make you stand out.

People Tree have filled the gap with a great tailored jacket and matching trousers, taking fair trade fashion away from its slouchy, crumpled comfort zone. And **Amana**, the label set up by two recent fashion graduates, Helen Wood and Erin Tabrar, using eco fabrics and fair trade working practices, could carve out a niche for itself doing cool clothes for city women. They already have a great trench, a pencil skirt, a crisp shirtdress and a well-cut jacket – so you can be city slick and sustainable too.

For really important meetings, you might want to enlist the services of a tailor (see page 26), or splash out on some elegant **Noir**, the Danish label making clothes that work for the catwalk as well as they do for the planet.

Dressing down: finding the perfect jeans

In the past year or so, there has been an explosion of eco denim, which means it's now incredibly easy to find the perfect pair of ethical jeans.

If you're a **Levis** fan, you'll love the new Eco jean. Levi's research showed that the customer (that's all of us) wanted an ethical option – that there was a demand for style, quality and sustainability. You see, we really do have the power to change the system!

For superior, standout style, it's worth taking a look at the independent brands making organic jeans hot, and leading the way in using fair practices in manufacture and production.

Nudie, the ultra-cool Swedish brand, is a name worth knowing. With an impeccable record in social responsibility, their organic cotton is spun, dyed, woven and finished using potato starch and indigo so that the process is chemical free. In fact, they are so fanatical about the finish of their unwashed denim that they recommend not washing it for six months (which makes perfect ecological sense).

Kuyichi jeans were founded by a Dutch fair trade initiative called Solidaridad, which uses Oro Blanco cotton from Peru. The farmers are partners in Kuyichi and share the profits. And the jeans themselves have a cool, lived-in look with loads of different fits from slouchy to skinny.

Ascension are based in the Derbyshire Peak District. Fairtrade certified, their jeans are made using organic cotton, with profits going towards building schools in India. The fit is great too.

Howies make organic denim jeans which, as with their whole range, attract a cult following.

Del-forte have all the makings of a regular premium It jean, complete with Hollywood fans and curvy cuts. Good that they are doing all the right things too, with organic denim, and their ReJEANeration project.

James Jeans make a high-end jean that is aged naturally rather than by chemicals mixing round in a washing machine for hours on end. An organic compound that includes green tea leaves and coffee is brushed onto the jeans and they are left out in the desert for two days to age gracefully on their own.

7 For All Mankind has introduced an organic jean, so if you are already a fan you don't have to swap brands.

Loomstate is the New York-based company set up by Rogan Gregory, making 100 per cent organic denim with some serious credibility – a jean even the denim anorak would consider buying.

How to Look Cool in Denim
By Rogan Gregory – co-founder of Loomstate Jeans and Edun's chief designer

* Make sure your ass looks good when you are saving someone else's.
* Avoid being a wasteful human being in all areas of life.
* You don't need an SUV. There are lots of other ways to prove

how big you are.
* Car pool, you will get there quicker.
* If you can live a little more efficiently, do it. It's about being responsible.
* Buy things, but make the right decision. We want to create jobs, but if you want a low carbon footprint, used clothing is great.
* It's tough when people dictate how we should behave. There are no answers. Everyone has a different answer. It depends on what you like to do.
* Slow down.
* It's a luxury to feel guilty because most of the world is just trying to survive.

Vintage sunglasses

Increasingly, designers look to the past for inspiration for their sunglasses. Four years ago, Simon Jablon, the son of sunglasses legend **Linda Farrow**, discovered a warehouse full of his mother's sunglasses that had been lying undiscovered for twenty to thirty years. She stopped designing sunglasses in the 1980s but left quite a legacy – almost every one of her frames is a classic. Some brands of sunglasses include vintage frames in their collections, including – most brilliantly edited – Cutler & Gross. They are recycling frames from just a few years ago, showing that what goes round always comes round again. See if you can beat them to it and discover some vintage sunnies of your own – but at bargain prices.

How to find and revamp old sunglasses
* You can find good sunglasses at the usual markets, like Brick Lane, Camden, charity shops and car boot sales. Don't forget to

look at old specs frames too – you might be able to convert them into shades with tinted lenses (and vice versa).

* To revamp an old pair, put the sunglasses in a bowl of hot (not boiling) water. Add washing-up liquid and leave to soak over-night – they will come up squeaky clean.

* To adjust sunglasses to fit, heat up the temples (the bit that goes behind the ears) with a hair dryer and bend slightly to adjust to your head.

* Sometimes vintage sunglasses can be hard to repair as the plastic is quite brittle or parts are not made any more. If in doubt, take them to your local optician just to have a look.

* To protect them, use a hard case, not a soft one.

Classic frames

Jackie O, Aviator and the Wayfarer are all timeless sunglasses – and will all make you feel like a superstar. Look out too for oversized frames or anything with a touch of the eccentric headmistress.

How to dress for a hot date

So you've got your silky underwear that nobody would ever guess was hemp; you've dabbed some organic L'Eau de Jatamansi by L'Artisan Parfumeur behind your ears, and you have a date for the night. But – the eternal question – what are you going to wear?

You don't want to go out looking ethically drab and shapeless. You are tempted to throw ethics to the breeze for a night. Comfort fashion would give out the wrong signal. But do not despair: I can definitely recommend a few ways to dress like a siren without setting off the alarms of the ethical fashion police.

* The first option, as always, is to go vintage. What could be more seductive than a 1960s cheongsam, or a fabulously sophisticated cocktail dress?
* If you want the vintage look but are worried about smelling of mothballs, match your outfit to your underwear and choose something slinky from Enamore.
* Go to American Apparel and opt for some clingy tubes of cotton Lycra, in colours to match your mood.
* Make sure your high heels are suitably fabulous. Beyond Skin will have something that will give your date something to talk about.
* Look out for vintage silk kimonos – just in case you have to slip into something more comfortable at home.

A Green Wedding

Perhaps I'm jumping the gun a little, but let's just imagine that the date went well. Really well . . . those hemp knickers were such a success that you are already hearing wedding bells. When Ruth Culver got married in 2005 she decided to make it a green wedding. She got so carried away with her own preparations that she has since become a wedding planner, passing on her expertise to a growing number of couples who want to make their ceremonies as waste free, responsible and chic as possible. Here's her step-by-step guide to planning an eco wedding:

The dress

Of course, looking fabulous on your wedding day is very important. It's only in the last century or so that a big, white confection became the norm for weddings, so you could simply invest in a stunning evening gown that you will enjoy wearing again. Other options are:

Vintage There's no better way to look unique and stylish, plus you get exquisite workmanship for a fraction of the price. If London is accessible there are plenty of antique emporia such as Vintage Modes in Mayfair and shops in the Portobello area. The Internet is a great resource and some suppliers take returns if the dress turns out not to be right. The best specialist suppliers are www.vintagedress.co.uk and www.vivalafrock.co.uk.

Re-modelling Very special emotions come into play when a bride wears a wedding dress previously worn by a loved one. Now that vintage fashions are all the rage, anything goes in terms of style. A good dressmaker can not only make size alterations but can completely re-model the dress, simply using the fabric to create something new.

Oxfam The queen of charity shops when it comes to wedding dresses, as they have a number of specialist bridal boutiques – for a list of locations see www.oxfam.org.uk/shop/highstreet/bridal. And don't expect dowdy cast-offs – you'll be amazed to discover that 95 per cent of their dresses are brand new, coming from catwalk shows and top boutiques. Only the finest donated dresses make it to their special shops (the remainder being sold in the high street). What could be better than knowing your bargain dress (average price is £250) has helped people in the developing world? Having your dress professionally cleaned and then donating it back afterwards is a lovely way to complete the eco circle.

Flowers

Most flowers are flown in from the other side of the world (where the workers are often not well protected from all the chemicals used) only for them to be thrown away after just one day. Instead, ask a florist to supply local flowers, or a nursery to grow exactly what you want. Better still, use plants – they live on and can be given as gifts, providing a lovely memento.

Catering
There are lots of options here. Local and seasonal produce reduces food miles and energy use. Organic helps minimise chemical impact on the land and on people. Naturally reared or free-range meat not only tastes better but will improve animal welfare. And for imported goods such as tea, coffee and sugar, fair trade means the farmers get paid a fair price. Ask for what you want – after all, you're paying the bill.

Venues
There are still very few specialist green or organic venues, though I'm sure it won't be long before this changes. Before you book your venue, ask the manager a few questions about their environmental policy – for example, what steps do they take to reduce energy and water consumption, recycle or compost their waste, and promote public transport?

Photography
Go digital – it uses far fewer chemicals than film. You only need the best few photographs as prints to frame: the rest can stay on disc, which is far more portable, plus you can put them online or email them across the world. Disposable cameras are obviously not a good idea – instead, ask your friends to email you copies of any pictures they took.

Travel
The single biggest environmental impact of a wedding is usually the honeymoon, with any stag/hen party flights just adding to the

burden. Think about finding a romantic bolthole in the UK – you'll be so tired after your wedding that you'll be delighted you don't have to tackle the exhaustions of an airport! Taking the train for a honeymoon in Europe is also a relaxing eco option, with the new super-fast routes making it all the more attractive. For further inspiration on great escapes, go to chapter 7.

Wedding list

Online, the Natural Collection have a wedding list service. But consider first, do you really require new stuff? Many couples already have what they need before they get married. There are plenty of charity wedding lists available as an alternative – some guests may be hesitant but explain how much it will mean to you and they will soon understand. My husband and I got back from our honeymoon to find a certificate saying that, among other things, a whole village in India had been vaccinated against river blindness. I can think of no better way to celebrate – we were moved to tears and it remains one of our most precious memories.

Confetti

Biodegradable confetti and dried petals are both available, or use linseed to give the birds a treat. Or ask a local florist for the flowers she's throwing out and pull off the petals – it looks stunning! For my wedding, fresh rose petals came from a friend's garden – she was delighted to be involved.

Invitations

The very green – and the ultra-modern – will want to email their invitations or create a complete online wedding site. If you're more of a traditionalist, opt for printed invitations, menus and so forth on recycled paper.

Rings

I am quite convinced that it will soon be just as desirable to have a vintage engagement ring as a vintage dress. There are some beautiful rings available so snap them up while they're still a fraction of the price of new. Alternatively, ask a designer to source conflict-free diamonds (the sale of new diamonds is often linked with wars and atrocities). For further inspiration, go to chapter 10.

How to make a wedding dress from a parachute

For a look straight from the heavens, few can rival Debbi Little's parachute dresses. Inspired by the make-do-and-mend war years – when the silk from parachutes was used to make wedding dresses – Debbi applies her own DIY punk ethic, and former training at Cerruti and Zandra Rhodes, to the task of creating the lightest, most fantastical of frocks.

There is something incredibly romantic about the idea of wearing a dress made out of an army surplus parachute. Debbi's ball gowns scrunch up into little bags – utilitarian and glamorous at the same time. 'I like the fact that I'm turning something with horrible connotations of war into something beautiful,' she says. 'It's a hard slog, making them look lovely. With recycled things, you have to make even more of an effort.' For more information, email debbilittlestudio106@yahoo.co.uk.

What to Wear to Make a Statement

If you want to get political, wear your heart on your chest, or simply draw attention to your best assets, then you should try a slogan T-shirt.

Slogan T-shirts have enjoyed a big comeback, with celebrities and fashionistas alike. Part of the 1980s revival, the movement wouldn't be complete without the return of Katharine Hamnett, whose '58% Don't Want Pershing' T-shirt – worn to meet Margaret Thatcher in 1984 – was a defining moment in political fashion history.

These days, there is a slogan T-shirt to fit every occasion, every mood, and every cause. You can get organic, fair trade, sweatshop-free ones from Sandbag (www.sandbag.uk.com) and Tonic T-shirts (www.tonictshirts.com). And if you can't find the slogan you want, you can always have one printed.

Here are my favourite five:

1. 'Corporate-bashing hippy-loving cause-fighting organic-eating Birkenstock-wearing campervan-touring life-affirming do-fucking-gooder' (Howies).
2. 'Will the world squeak when the oil runs out?' (Greenfibres).
3. 'Save the earth, it's the only planet with chocolate on it' (Greenfibres).
4. 'Clean up or Die' (Katharine Hamnett, 1989 re-issue).
5. 'Grow some vegetables' (Howies).

To print your very own

Green is the New Black T-shirt,

simply log on to

www.greenisthenewblack.typepad.com

and follow the instructions.

4

DIY Style

DIY Style

'One should either be a work of art, or wear a work of art'

Oscar Wilde

Once you've mastered the basics of reinvention, it's time to get creative. The high art of DIY style is being able to spot the potential in clothes, to find items that aren't quite right – that are dated or ill-fitting, faded and unloved – and transform them into desirable and fabulous must-haves. Of course this takes more than just a good eye; it takes skill and time, or, for the time-pushed green goddess, knowing where to go to get the look . . .

How to Save Money and Look Fabulous

Shopping with a conscience does not necessarily mean buying things on the cheap, but it is rewarding to know how to dress decently and save money in the process. And there is great satisfaction to be had from finding a new outfit for nothing – not dissimilar to the thrill of bagging a bargain at Primark.

The thriftiest way to high fashion is to make your own. Our mothers' generation – and their mothers before them – made clothes all the time. I remember all my party dresses as a small child were homemade. We used to buy packs of fabric squares – all different colours and patterns – which meant there was an endless supply of interesting materials around the house.

When I reached age ten, I had a thing about circular skirts. I played the soundtrack to *American Graffiti* non-stop and thought I was a teddy girl. So my mum made a pattern for a circular skirt – it was literally a circle of fabric with a hole in the middle for my waist. I had lots of them. That was the thing about making your own clothes: you could have as many as you could make. The skirts would fly out when I spun around, my hair tied up in a high ponytail.

As a teenager, I learnt how to make clothes of my own, and even started to design them myself. I would spend just as much time in the haberdashery department of John Lewis as I did in Chelsea Girl, shopping for matching outfits with my girlfriend. I would buy patterns, but I was more interested in the finished result than the making itself. I wanted instant gratification, and learnt how to cut corners – how to alter patterns to simplify them and speed the process up. I recall lying on the floor and drawing around myself on a few pieces of newspaper, and somehow constructing dresses and skirts from my own silhouette. Bondaweb – the stuff you iron on to make a hem so that you don't have to sew it – came in very handy.

I became quite expert at making ra-ra skirts and batwing tops. And any leftover fabric would come in handy for tying round my head in a big bow. I might have looked like raggedy Ann, but it was great fun. I could make a different outfit every Saturday – often in a matter of hours. To me, it was what fashion was all about.

These days, haberdashery departments have moved from prime location on the ground floor of department stores to an obscure corner somewhere impossible to find. And they are now seen as the sole preserve of older women, making sensible blouses, or WI stalwarts. It's a shame, because all those reels of ribbon and trimmings, stacks of coloured net (underskirts were so easy to make, and net came in the best of neon colours), cards of buttons, embroidery silks, and different prints were such an inspiration.

When I finally did arrive at St Martins, I discovered the fabric shops of Berwick Street in Soho. These were places used by 'the trade' and you felt you really had to know what you were talking about before you stepped inside. They seemed to sell just about any fabric imaginable – and often at very good prices.

Borovicks still has mythical status for me, as does Kleins, the wonderful shop that is dedicated to trimmings – every clothing customiser's idea of paradise. V V Rouleaux is the upmarket version, but I still prefer the more basic surroundings of Kleins, which is pretty much unchanged since it opened in 1936. These days though, you can buy online, and it seems to sell just about anything you could ever possibly need.

The thing about making your own clothes is that it takes a little time and sometimes a lot of imagination. But it opens up the possibilities of what you can wear, and means that you will always stand out from the crowd. You know when you walk into a room that nobody else will be wearing the same thing as you. In some cases, they probably wouldn't want to either, but that's another matter altogether.

Best for buttons and bits

Borovicks: www.borovickfabricsltd.co.uk
Kleins: www.kleins.co.uk
V V Rouleaux: www.vvrouleaux.com
Button Queen: www.thebuttonqueen.co.uk
Sew Hip: www.sewhip.co.uk

The web has filled the gap left by the closing of the haberdashery departments, and is introducing a new generation to crafts and particularly to dressmaking. What could be finer than to do something creative and tactile when you come home from a day spent in front of a computer screen?

Download a dress

Lisa Howdin is a 37-year-old from Canberra, Australia. In 2005, she set up her own online business – the fantastic www.fitz patterns.com – selling dress patterns to download from the web. Her site features a number of free patterns, including a simple A-line wrap skirt that she estimates will take just two hours to make. Basically, and without having to queue for the fitting room, you can make it in the time it would take you to get into town and buy one from a chain store.

Make your own McQueen, Galliano or Margiela

For absolutely no charge whatsoever, you can try your hand at a bit of a designer masterpiece. Download the patterns below at Nick Knight's fantastic Show Studio website:

* Alexander McQueen Kimono Jacket:
  www.showstudio.com/projects/ddlmcqueen/download.html
* Unfinished Martin Margiela:
  www.showstudio.com/projects/ddl_margiela/download.html
* John Galliano Pirate Jacket:
  www.showstudio.com/projects/unf/unf_start.html

An Antoni & Alison skirt to cut out and keep

Antoni & Alison say they mean well. And they really do. While they are yet to use organic cotton for their T-shirts, they like to encourage a little DIY at home, and have kindly agreed to share their very easy skirt pattern so that you can make it yourself – preferably out of some old fabric you've collected, or something you want to recycle.

If you want the full Antoni & Alison experience (and who doesn't?) you can order their own fabric by the metre from www.antoniandalison.co.uk (there are three prints to choose from – egg, screwed-up paper, or porridge flower) and choose a set of pin labels, complete with safety pins, to finish it all off perfectly. 'I hate my skirt' might be a good one. Or 'Don't spend any more money'. And just to show they really are serious about you trying out your sewing skills (as well as doing a bit of making do and mending), they have a sewing kit complete with buttons!

So here it is, your very own Antoni & Alison skirt to cut out and keep . . .

Antoni & Alison Square Skirt, Size 10
(Add 5 cm overall for each size up)

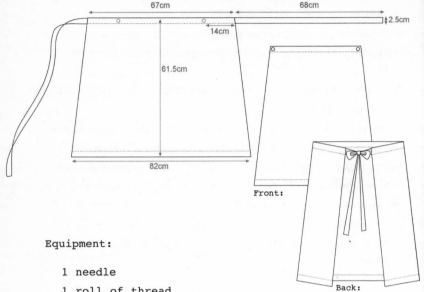

Front:

Back:

Equipment:

- 1 needle
- 1 roll of thread
- 2 'Antoni & Alison' buttons
- 2 poppers
- 1 'Antoni & Alison' label
- 2 metres of one-metre-wide 'Antoni & Alison' fabric

Instructions:

* Enlarge the pattern above on to paper to the correct size.
* Cut out front and back adding a 1 cm seam allowance on side seams and a 2.5 cm seam allowance at waist and hem.
  The front and back pattern pieces are exactly the same.

* You will also need to cut out four strips of
  fabric for the ties.
  You will need two strips for each tie.
* Place the fabric strips back to back and sew the
  edges together, leaving one end open to turn the
  ties the correct way out.
* The ties should measure 2.5 cm x 68 cm when
  finished.
* These ties should then be sewn into the side seams
  of the skirt at the top.
* Sew the side seams of the skirt together, not
  forgetting to include the ties.
  Then turn up the hem, and turn over the waistband
  to create a neat finish.
* You now need to attach the buttons and poppers for
  the fastening.
* Sew on a button 14 cm away from the side seam on
  the outside of the skirt on each side, as
  decoration (please see diagram above).
* Then, directly behind that button, on the inside
  of the skirt, place one side of the popper and sew
  on. Do this on each side behind each button.
* You will then need to attach the other side of the
  popper to the inside of the back of the skirt,
  again 14 cm from the side seam.

You are now finished and can wear your Antoni &
Alison skirt with pride!

TIP:
Why not contrast the front and back with different
fabrics. Choose two of your favourite Antoni &
Alison prints and you can wear them either way
round.

Girls with Purls

Cast Off are on a mission to get the world knitting. The duo, Rachael Matthews and Louise Harries, recently opened their first shop, Prick Your Finger, in London's Bethnal Green. It has everything you need to be 'an ornamental hermit, or to make the best party costumes'. They believe an original look, well worn, is priceless. To start you off, here is a pattern for beginners.

How to knit a fluffy pompom ankle bracelet from your pet rabbit's wool
By Cast Off

First you'll need a pet rabbit (or alternatively, borrow a friend's). The breed to look for is angora, on account of their beautiful, supersoft angora wool. They can be lots of different colours, and there are different breeds. Ours is called Rfid and he is a pretty white, with hints of pink through his wool. Angora rabbits need to be brushed every other day, and given a haircut about four times a year. Cared for properly, your bunny could probably give you enough wool to knit a small jumper every year, but it is best to stick to small things like tea cosies.

Equipment:
The wool is baby fine so it's best to mix the angora with 30 per cent Shetland wool, as it needs a slightly tougher fibre to get it to spin.

It's probably best to use fine needles, like a 3 or 3.5.

Instructions:
1. Make your pompoms using the potato masher method (as illustrated). Basically, you wrap quite a lot of yarn around the

masher, make two very tight ties, and then cut between the ties. You need about sixteen pompoms per ankle, preferably all different colours.

2. Thread them all together with a needle and thread.

3. Attach ribbons or French knitting to the ends and decorate with bells.

If you need a bit of help, there is a cooperative in Yorkshire where you can send your bunny fur to get it spun, weighed and sent back to you. Our angora rabbit came from: Llynfi Textiles, www.llynfitextiles.co.uk, and they will be happy to offer any help and advice you need. 🙶

How to make a recycled apron (with or without ra-ra frills)
By Lovelylovely

To look every inch the domestic goddess, you'll need:

* Approximately one metre of curtain/tablecloth fabric
* Scraps of a contrasting fabric, for bias binding
* Threads
* One sewing machine or sewing kit
* Pinking shears (optional)

Instructions:

1. Cut out fabric pieces as in fig (a) adding a 1 cm seam allowance.

fig (a)

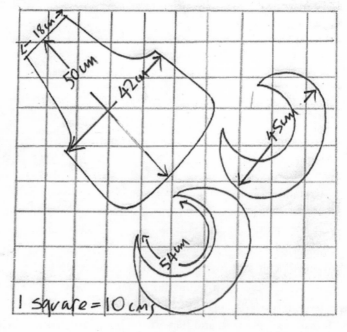

2. To make apron bib, hem side seams and hem.
3. To make bias binding, cut diagonal strips of fabric 3 cm wide. Sew the different strips together with a diagonal seam as in fig (b). Make your strip 3–4 metres long. Fold over 0.5 cm along edges and iron flat as shown.

fig (b)

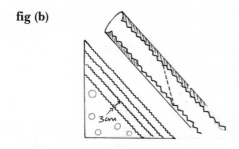

4. To make frills, sew the bias binding along outer edge of frill. Then make some tucks in frills so that the top of the frill length fits across the apron width, as in fig (c).

fig (c)

5. Assemble. Sew frills to apron skirt as in fig (d). Sew a binding across the top of the apron bib. Sew a binding to make apron strings and neck loop as in fig (d). Knot some beads from bracelets/necklaces to the apron string ends.

fig (d)

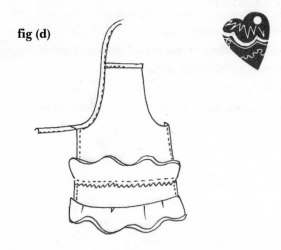

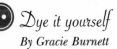

Dye it yourself
By Gracie Burnett

Using ingredients from the kitchen cupboard, vegetable patch and even your local park, natural dyeing is great fun, and a really simple and exciting process. Here are a few of my favourite ways of making colour (for more, go to www.gracieburnett.com).

To keep things simple, the following recipes make up enough to dye two metres of light fabric. Silk and wool work best, but you could experiment first on old T-shirts.

* One pair of Marigold gloves or similar
* A couple of longish sticks, or long-handled spoons, for stirring
* One Pyrex jug
* A couple of old metal spoons
* Muslin bags like the ones used for jam making
* A jam pan, or the largest pan in your kitchen
* One big bucket (big enough to hold the fabric, without it being too squashed up)
* Measuring scales

Step One

Firstly you must wash the fabric. I normally do this on the fastest programme in the machine. I always use a pH-balanced detergent. Ecover or similar is perfect. It makes sense to wash by hand if you are only dyeing a very small amount. After washing, leave the fabric in a bucket with a little water in it, making sure it can't dry out.

Step Two

Because you're using a natural dye, you'll need a mordant (or chemical compound) to fix your colour to the cloth. Alum is the most useful mordant. It's very cheap, you can use it on all fabrics, and it helps the dyes create a much brighter, more vibrant colour.

Check out the online suppliers of alum in the box on page 94.

Ingredients: 4 ounces alum, 1 ounce cream of tartar

Fill your jam pan about half-full with water, pop it on the hob and heat until boiling. Next pour some of the water into the Pyrex jug and dissolve the alum and cream of tartar in this. Once dissolved, add the liquid to the pot and stir well. After about five minutes add the fabric and bring the pan to a simmer. Keep like this for about 30–45 minutes, stirring occasionally. Take off heat and leave to cool. Remove the fabric carefully, squeezing out as much of the excess water as possible. Pop it in a bucket, with a little bit of water to stop it drying out. It is safe to throw the mordant water down the drain, as all the alum will be absorbed into the cloth.

Step Three
The fabric is now ready for the dye pot!

Recipe for the summer: shades of orange and yellow rusts

Ingredients: Onion skins

We all use onions in our cooking, but the great news is that you can also use the skins of red and white onions for yellow dyes. Every time you a chop an onion, keep the skins. Put them in a paper bag and leave them somewhere dry. If in a rush, you can use the skins straightaway as well. I would suggest that about three good handfuls of onion skins will be plenty for the dye pot.

Pop your pan on the hob, half to three-quarters full of water. Simply add the onion skins, and bring the pot to the simmer. You will notice that the water turns a dark, yellow, rust colour. Lower the temperature a bit and add the fabric to the pan, squeezing it as you lower it into the pot. Squeezing or stirring is important if you want to get an even shade.

Now it's up to you. You can leave your fabric in as long as you like, depending on the colour you want. The more you leave it the more rust-like the colour will become. When you have achieved the colour you want, take the fabric out and wash it with a little bit of detergent until the water runs clear. Hey presto, you have a wonderful yellow.

Depending on the strength of your dye pot, the fabric can change colour quite quickly and you might be tempted to take it out too soon. But trust me, leave it in a bit longer and you will end up with a beautiful, rich, golden yellow.

Recipe for the vintage look: shades of brown and taupe

Ingredients: Tea bags

Dyeing with tea is really easy, and perfect for an old white T-shirt that has gone that horrible shade of white. The thing about tea is that every brand and type has a different strength, so you might want to experiment a bit. Cheap tea tends to be stronger than the more fancy teas, so Tetley is a good place to start. Earl Grey is a winner too. And that's just the beginning: raspberry tea will give the fabric a pinkish colour, Orange Pekoe, an orangey colour that gets darker over time, and so on.

Fill your pan about three-quarters full and add to this about twenty new tea bags or forty used ones. Alternatively, use three to four ounces of loose-leaf tea (less if the leaves were used for the tea pot at breakfast). Put the leaves in a muslin bag and tie it up first, so nothing can escape. Next, heat the pot up and bring it to a gentle simmer. The simple rule of thumb here is the longer you leave the pot, the stronger the dye will become. When you think you have a good deep colour, take out the tea bags (and the muslin bag), and dispose of them in the garden. Tea is a great source of nitrogen, and the worms love a nibble too!

Turn the heat down and add your fabric, squeezing the fabric as you lower it into the pan. When you are happy with the colour, remove, rinse, dry and wear! Remember, tea has a lot of tannin in it, and if you want to pass the shirt or T-shirt down as an heirloom, it probably won't make it. Over time, the tannins will slowly eat away at the fabric and eventually destroy it – talk about recycling!

Online suppliers of mordants, dyes and specialised equipment:

P & M Woolcraft (www.pmwoolcraft.co.uk).
Fibrecrafts (www.fibrecrafts.com).
Essential reading for the novice dyer: *Wild Colour* by Jenny Dean.

Make Do and Mend

Make do and mend was the mantra of an entire generation of women who lived through the war. There were make-do-and-mend classes, to teach you how to make a pillowcase into a baby's dress, a skirt from a pair of dad's old trousers, or a blouse or dress from a parachute. Old curtains were cut up to make skirts and dresses. Unwanted jumpers were unravelled and knitted into something else. It was considered unpatriotic not to patch your jumpers or darn your socks. The Board of Trade issued pamphlets with titles such as 'Go Through Your Wardrobe – Make Do and Mend', 'Don't Boil Woollens', 'Better Wear from Your Shoes', 'New Life for Old Sheets', and 'Do You Care for Clothes?'

While no one is advocating the return of clothes rationing

(although a slight reduction in the quantities we buy wouldn't hurt any of us), we can learn a lot from our grandparents about how to look after our clothes and make them last longer. The time it takes to sew on a button or darn a hole in a jumper is a fraction of what it will take to go out and buy a new one. And it's far more satisfying.

Some wartime tips to make your granny proud

* Mend and make do to save buying new.

* Outdoor clothes will wear better and last much longer if you change them as soon as you get home, and if you sponge them and iron them occasionally. Keep special clothes for the house, the garden, the city etc., and wear them alternately. All your clothes will then be fresher.

* Reproof your raincoat by rubbing beeswax over the inside and then ironing it with a hot iron.

* Beware of moths, particularly between September and spring. Keep a look-out for moth eggs in all of your clothes, not just wool. At least once a month, brush and shake your clothes and open cupboard doors to let the sunlight in. Scrub out cupboards and drawers regularly.

* Put wet shoes on shoetrees as soon as you take them off and stuff the toes with tissue paper. Leather looks like new when treated with sour milk (sounds gross, I know) rubbed in with a piece of cheesecloth.

* Brown shoes always look polished if rubbed each morning with the inside skin of a banana. Leave them to dry and then polish them with a piece of dry rag.

Styling surgery

If you really don't fancy 'doing it yourself', one company that can help is the east London duo **Junky Styling**. Friends Kerry Seager and Annika Sanders started out making their own clothes for going out clubbing in the early 1990s. These days, they are London's premier recycled clothing company with a shop off Brick Lane and two collections a year for London Fashion Week (clothes that will work for that season, but can also be worn for seasons to come). They believe in recycling for our future and giving old or worn-out clothes a new lease of life.

While their raw material remains the same – clothing that has been thrown or given away – the secret to their success is that they keep an eye on new trends and fashion. They're just girls who love dressing up and they do that in a way that is original and sustainable, diverting textiles from landfill and back into pride of place in your wardrobe.

Tips from Junky Styling

If you are a fan of vintage dresses and coats befriend a well-dressed old granny (preferably with no living relatives and a similar size to you) and be so much more than just the granddaughter she never had! She'll probably need help going through the treasures in her wardrobe and maybe the boxes of ball gowns in the attic. You must be prepared to go to Bingo and perform home perms.

To recapture that 80s vibe and stay warm by finding a soft old jumper (lambswool or cashmere) with slim arms and cut very carefully around the armhole, cutting close to the seam to create leg warmers. Alternatively, you can cut off at the elbow and make a hole in each of the seams on the rib cuffs for your thumbs, and you have fingerless glove-style arm cuffs.

Learn to sew on a button (see page 30) – this is so helpful when shopping. For example, if you fall in love with a jacket but you feel the shape of it may be a little 'boxy' on your figure, try wrapping it around your waist and see how the shape would improve if the buttons were sewn on a bit further across.

T-shirts don't fray, which means you can chop the necks into different shapes and make vests by cutting off arms. Make strategic slashes all over T-shirts to really mess them up, but remember to pull on each slash to create nice curved edges to each cut mark.

Don't be too hasty to throw your old clothes out, especially if they are good-quality fabric. Junky Styling can deconstruct and reconstruct virtually anything and create wonderful new garments for you as part of their Wardrobe Surgery service. A jacket can become a fully boned basque or pencil skirt, or a dress can become a top very simply; every single operation is unique to the customer.

Fashionably wasted

If you're looking for luxury, Orsola de Castro is a London-based Italian designer whose business is making something out of nothing. Her company, **From Somewhere**, was started in 1997, when she began reworking worn-out cashmere, embellishing the holes with decorative crochet work. She went on to work with the high street chain Jigsaw, customising their rejected knitwear and making it saleable.

Orsola's whole ethos is to save clothing and material from needless waste. 'What happens to the fashion industry's waste at the end of each season?' she asks. 'In the realms of high fashion, where a few metres of beautiful silk can cost hundreds of pounds, it ends up in the bin and then in landfill.' Determined to stop the rot, Orsola recycles the scraps and waste from some of Italy's finest fabric mills, creating well-designed garments patched together out of the best quality, woven textiles in the world. 'I recycle the rubbish from the big designers,' she says. 'Companies like Brioni are fully aware that I'm using their waste.'

She has even worked with the Italian sportswear company Kappa, making cocktail dresses out of their waste football and cycling shirts. The factories and fabric mills welcome the fact that she is making use of their off-cuts. And, of course, Orsola gets to use the sort of high-quality fabrics she could only dream of being able to afford as a small designer.

While Orsola is passionate about sustainable style (and relieving rubbish tips), she is also, first and foremost, a great designer. Her latest collection is Holly Hobby meets Studio 54 – a unique blend of grown-up sophistication with make do and mend – which is why her first shop has just opened on Westbourne Grove in west London.

Traid secrets

As you know, there are plenty of ways to recycle your cast-offs. But one of the best routes, in the UK at least, is to drop your spoils into the big green recycling bins dotted around London, the Midlands and Brighton. These belong to Traid, a fantastically innovative charity, committed to protecting the environment, reducing poverty, and generally bringing good to the world, through recycling. By collecting and selling our reclaimed clothing, Traid make a business out of the mainstream industry's waste and, in so doing, they help fund sustainable development projects in some of the poorest regions of the world.

Determined to find out more (and perhaps bag myself a bargain in the process), I went along to the charity's recycling depot, in the shadow of the new Wembley Stadium.

'People put all sorts of things in our bins,' says Enedina Columbano, who manages the place. 'We've had an urn of ashes and dead cats, but we've also had a fantastic Gucci dress.' The donations vary of course, depending on location, with the better-heeled parts of town yielding some real treasures.

I keep my eyes peeled. There are cages of clothes everywhere, all at different stages of the process. As soon as new deliveries arrive, they are emptied on to a conveyor belt in the middle of the space and a team sets to work, sorting the riches from the rubbish.

In just a few minutes, I see a good denim jacket, as well as a Gucci handbag being tossed into the buyer's crate. 'I think it's a fake,' says Enedina. She has a well-trained eye. The real thing does turn up once in a while but, on closer inspection, this is indeed a copy. Still, someone will enjoy reusing it, especially if they think they've got a real Gucci bag for a few pounds.

The Traid workers usually have a fashion background. 'You have to love clothes to work with them eight hours a day,' says Enedina. Two tantalisingly empty boxes have the Harrods logo on them. Occasionally, big stores will send unsold stock – usually with labels cut out. For Traid, and ultimately the customers, this is bonanza time.

What's interesting about Traid is that it is like a microcosm of the fashion industry. The shops sell stock targeted at their different clientele. London's Westbourne Grove store is the smartest, and the choice pieces will usually end up there – at premium prices. Brixton has diverse and fashionable core customers who will snap up the more interesting, creative pieces. And Holloway is aimed at the more everyday consumer. This is where the bread-and-butter clothes will end up, with coats selling for around £10 and the average price being £3.50. The managers all know what their customers want and buy accordingly – just like the buyers for any high street chain. And the stock changes according to the seasons, with sales at the end of summer and winter and new stock every week.

As well as providing stock for the shops, there is also a Traid Remade project that has been going since 2001. A small team of designers, led by Tracey Cliffe, is allowed to forage in the bin devoted to fabrics and trimmings, and to take away clothes that are really on their last legs. These are then remade into new garments that are as desirable as something you might see in a vintage shop, or on the rails at Topshop. Nothing is wasted. And the designs look incredibly fresh.

Tracey has been making and customising clothes since she was thirteen. Nowadays, she can transform real rubbish – an old sweatshirt, tatty curtains, a man's shirt – into a fashionable new dress, in just forty-five minutes. To keep prices low, it is important that the clothes can be made simply and quickly, so she's learnt to sew fast. Her tiny office is kitted out with two domestic sewing machines (salvaged from the recycling bins), and boxes upon boxes of rescued zips, buttons and trimmings.

In 2005, Traid Remade enlisted the help of around twenty designers, including Betty Jackson and Wayne Hemingway, to use raw materials in the Traid warehouse to make their own designs. These were then sold on eBay for the charity. Occasionally Traid host fashion shows too, with the remade clothes – all unique one-offs – reflecting current trends. For more information, and details of your nearest Traid shop, see www.traid.org.uk

Remake it yourself

When you study the basic shape of a T-shirt, and in particular the fabric that it's made of, you realise the potential of an old one that has lost its shape but still holds a place in your heart.

How to make a T-shirt into a halter top
By Junky Styling

1. Fold the T-shirt so that the armholes line up, creating a crease down the front and down the back of the garment.

2. Cut all the way down the back centre crease and open out.

3. Cut under the neckline from both sides, leaving about 15 cm in the centre at the front.

4. Cut out the shoulder and sleeve sections to just below the armholes. (Tip: do one side, fold over and use the cut lines as a template for the other side.)

5. To create back straps, measure 15 cm down the remaining side seams and 5 cm up from the bottom, and remove these side sections. (Tip: pulling on the remaining straps gives them curly, raw edges.)

6. Cut straight down the front centre crease to create a v-neck. Tie the straps at the top and bottom, and voila!

How to make a rubbish old T-shirt into a slinky shift dress
By Tracey Cliffe of Traid Remade

1. You need at least two T-shirts, preferably big ones: steal your dad's/brother's/boyfriend's, or you could get away with one lady's and one man's.

2. The top of the dress needs to fit you relatively snugly. If you're using two big T-shirts one of them needs to be cut to fit the female form. To do this cut up both sides of the shirt, following the line around the armholes to make a mini, sleeveless version of the original.

3. Re-sew the sides together, and cut off the bottom of the T-shirt, just under your boobs.

4. With the other T-shirt, cut off the sleeves and neck so you have one big rectangle. Alternatively, cut into a long trapezium shape if you want the dress to have more of a 60s swingy feel.

5. Attach the rectangle of T-shirt to the 'top of the dress' that you cut out earlier. The rectangle should be wider, so you'll need to put a few pinches or pleats in to fit – this also gives the dress a better shape.

6. If the fancy takes you, you could sew some buttons on to the top half, maybe fashion a collar. Why, you could even attach some big pockets on the front to store away all your sewing essentials. The possibilities are almost endless!

Recycling: the facts

* It is estimated that more than one million tonnes of textiles are thrown away every year, with most of this coming from household sources. Textiles make up about 3 per cent by weight of a household bin. At least 50 per cent of the textiles we throw away are recyclable.

* Textiles present particular problems in landfill. Synthetic or man-made fibres do not decompose, while woollen garments will decompose but produce methane gas, which contributes to global warming.

* If everyone in the UK bought one reclaimed woollen garment each year, it would save an average of 371 million gallons of water (the average UK reservoir holds about 300 million gallons) and 480 tonnes of chemical dyestuffs.

* Over 70 per cent of the world's population use second-hand clothes.

* It is estimated that only 6 per cent of materials donated to charity shops ends up in landfill (Association of Charity Shops).

How to Wash Your Clothes

Caring for your clothes once you've spent so much time making them (or so much money buying them) is really crucial if you want to reduce the overall carbon emissions of your wardrobe. As I write, I have to confess that the tumble-drier is whirring away. It's a windy day, but it's too cold to hang the washing on the line. It's making me feel guilty. I can envisage the electricity meter spinning. Not only is this costing me money, it is spilling more CO_2 into the atmosphere. The more I think about it, the more I know I am going to have to turn off the tumble-drier. But, probably like you, I am used to life's conveniences.

My mother's generation coped perfectly well without tumble-driers. I remember growing up when rainy days at home could mean only one thing: knickers, bras, Y-fronts and pyjamas strewn shamelessly over every available radiator surface. I suppose this still wasn't saintly conduct, as the heating would be cranked up high. But on fine days, the clothes would be outside, blowing in the wind, making full use of the natural resources. We have grown so used to life at the press of a button . . .

There! I've done it! I turned off the drier and hung the clothes out to dry. I feel as if I've done something positive. I've been outside and a bit of fresh air is just the thing. I'm ignoring the fact that the clouds are turning grey and it is suddenly about to rain.

According to researchers at Cambridge University, 60 per cent of the carbon emissions generated by a simple cotton T-shirt comes from the twenty-five washes and machine dryings it will require in its life. Washing clothes less frequently and at lower temperatures will not make you smell like a soap dodger. And even though there are experiments afoot to create fabrics that clean themselves or don't need to be washed, it's really much more appealing to wash clothes in soap and water, rather than giving them a wipe clean. Still, there are ways to reduce your clothing carbon emissions.

Tips for a caring wash

* Wash at thirty degrees. Around 1.6 billion kilowatt-hours of energy are wasted annually by washing at the traditional forty degrees.
* Line dry your clothes wherever possible.
* Learn to love polyester – it might be naughty for the planet when it's made, but items can be washed on lower temperatures and hardly take any time to dry.
* Always use eco-friendly detergents, like Ecover or Bio-D.
* Invest in eco balls. They go into your wash instead of detergent. Apparently they produce ionised oxygen that activates the water molecules naturally, allowing them to penetrate deep into fibres for a natural clean. Sounds a bit like soap dodging to me. But at three pence per wash, they are surely worth a try: see www.ecotopia.co.uk.
* Use Soap Pods. Another strange one this: soap pods grow on trees and you can use each pod three times, for natural cleaning without any nasties: see www.soapods.com.

How to dry clean green

Don't you just hate it when you buy clothes and discover they are 'dry clean only' when you come to wash them? Traditional dry cleaning chemicals are nasty and carcinogenic, and really no good for you, or the planet. Plus, I object to spending more than the price of a Primark dress every time I want to get fresh.

A lot of the time, the 'dry clean only' label is simply a way of covering up for the fact that the item is such poor quality that it won't survive a vigorous wash. I tend to ignore the label and give things a gentle wash by hand. This can be risky though.

If you do need to use the services of a dry cleaner, there are cleaner, greener options. Green Earth Cleaning (www.greenearth cleaning.com) is an alternative dry cleaning system that uses silica rather than the traditional chemicals. If you are lucky, your local branch of Johnsons will offer the service, and if they don't, pester them until they do.

5

Can Celebrities Save the World?

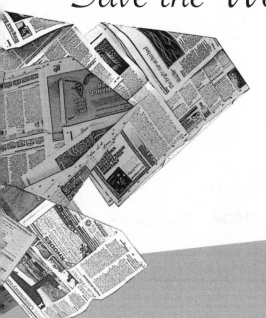

Can Celebrities Save the World?

'So we find ourselves on the brink. It's clear humans have had a devastating impact on our planet's ecological way of life. Because we've waited, because we've turned our backs on nature's warning signs, and because our political and corporate leaders have consistently ignored the overwhelming scientific evidence, the challenges we face are that much more difficult. We are in the environmental age whether we like it or not'

Leonardo DiCaprio, *The 11th Hour*

Welcome to Hollywood: the Emerald City

You know there's something in the air when Tinseltown decides to get in on the act. Green is the latest storyline to hit Hollywood. Al Gore's *An Inconvenient Truth* galvanised the movement, and Leo DiCaprio has become the star of the show. His film *The 11th Hour* is set to make global warming the hottest topic of conversation since, well, conflict diamonds.

At Robert Redford's Sundance Film Festival 2007, there was a whole area dedicated to green issues. Showing shorts about the environment, it boasted its own celebrity panel, including reconstructed hippy Daryl Hannah, and Laura Dern. The American Pavilion at Cannes went carbon neutral for the first time by buying carbon offsets from Native Energy. Even the actual business of filmmaking is having an overhaul.

When you think of Hollywood, you think big blockbusters, edge-of-your-seat explosions, big budgets and excess-all-areas. The entertainment industry annually generates over 140,000 tonnes of ozone and diesel pollutants from trucks, generators and special effects alone. Private jets, Airstream, and helicopter rides are just the tip of the ever-decreasing iceberg. But the industry is changing fast. In 2004, *The Day After Tomorrow* became the first film to be declared carbon neutral, after Twentieth Century Fox paid $200,000 for a reforestation project to offset some 10,000 tonnes of carbon dioxide emissions. And since *An Inconvenient Truth*, the standard has been set, with studios actually employing experts to look after recycling, sustainability issues, and social corporate responsibility.

Of course the real power to change the moviemaking world comes from the stars, and it seems that enough of them are getting serious about the environment. Cameron Diaz insisted on a Green Seal (awarded by the Environmental Media Association to productions that meet with its eco standards) for her film *In Her Shoes*. In the future, she and others like her might start to demand that carbon neutrality is written into their contracts. No doubt it won't be long before it will be added to the end credits, along with 'no animals were harmed in the making of this film'.

The new anti-global-warming organisation Global Cool has enlisted celebrity support to beat climate change. Its goal is to convince one billion people to reduce their carbon emissions by just one tonne a year, for the next ten years – which scientists hope might be enough to avoid the climatic tipping point. Josh Hartnett, KT Tunstall, Pink, The Killers, Razorlight (who recently recorded their first solar-powered single for Friends of the Earth) and Sienna Miller have all thrown their weight behind the effort.

Brad Pitt and Orlando Bloom have gone one step further, and built green houses. Bloom says his new London pad is 'as green as I can make it. It's got solar panels on the roof, energy-efficient lightbulbs – newer technology basically that is environmentally friendly. It might not be possible for everyone to live a completely green lifestyle, but we can do little things to help slow global warming.' And it's the little details that are beginning to count everywhere: Charlize Theron is demanding organic makeup on the set of her new film (all reportedly from www.alchemists apprentice.com). Teri Hatcher was spotted holidaying in a solar-powered eco trailer on an organic farm. And Cameron Diaz is finishing off writing her how-to eco manual, *The Green Book*, with contributions and tips from everyone from Justin Timberlake to Jennifer Aniston.

What's great about all of this is that where Hollywood leads, the rest of us tend to follow. Who cares about politicians? The real power to change people's attitudes and lifestyles is with our celebrities. And for every Paris Hilton, with her gas-guzzling Mercedes and her serial handbag habit, there is an Angelina Jolie or a Scarlett Johansson – role models who are cool *and* care.

Care in the community: the Hollywood A list

Leonardo DiCaprio

Leo really has come into his own as an environmentalist with more power than many politicians. He is a man on a mission. His excellent eco site (www.leonardodicaprio.org) gives news and short films, offers advice and tells you how to get involved. His documentary *The 11th Hour* takes up where Al Gore's *An Inconvenient Truth* left off.

He says: 'Global warming is not only the number one environmental challenge we face today, but one of the most important issues facing all of humanity. We all have to do our part to raise awareness about global warming and the problems we as a people face in promoting a sustainable environmental future for our planet's future.'

Established in 1998, the Leonardo DiCaprio Foundation has actively fostered awareness of environmental issues through participation with such organisations as Natural Resources Defense Council, Global Green, USA, the International Fund for Animal Welfare, and National Geographic Kids, to name a few.

Natalie Portman

A vegetarian since the age of eight (no wonder she loves Beyond Skin shoes) Natalie Portman has long been an advocate of environmental causes. She even joined an environmental song-and-dance troupe at the age of twelve. In 2005 she travelled to Uganda, Guatemala and Ecuador as the Ambassador of Hope for Finca International, an organisation that promotes micro-lending to help finance women-owned businesses in poor countries. Before her visits, she said, 'I wasn't even aware that two-thirds of the world population are extremely poor, living on less than a dollar a day, and that 70 per cent of those people are women and children. It's not something they teach you in school in the States.'

Thandie Newton

Brought up in Cornwall, Thandie retains some of her West Country ethics, and after swapping her BMW for a Prius, recommended that her celebrity friends do the same. Environmentally and socially aware, she wins extra Brownie points for crocheting Christmas presents for her family and friends.

Daryl Hannah

In her blonde pigtails and organic denims, Daryl makes going wild in the country look very cool. A serious environmentalist who built her own solar-powered eco home off the grid in the Rockies, her blog (www.dhlovelife.com) promotes living harmoniously with the planet and reverence for the interconnectedness of all living things. She recently said, 'I don't want to buy eco jeans made by slave labour, or chocolate harvested by kidnapped children, any more than biofuels from slash-and-burn operations or imported from halfway around the world.' You go, Daryl!

Maggie Gyllenhaal

An anti-war protestor, and all-round cool gal, Maggie's quirky style has that thrown-together look that might have come from thrift stores, just as easily as from Prada. She wears both with the same laid-back style.

Mischa Barton

She may look like someone seriously addicted to over-consumption but Mischa says that, at times, she'd rather stay at home and read Dostoevsky than go shopping. A modern style icon, in June 2007 she fronted Traid's temporary fashion swap shop in Knightsbridge, London. Designers including Phoebe Philo, Alice Temperley and Philip Treacy donated pieces, while Barton parted with her Roberto Cavalli linen shorts, a vintage Eagles tour T-shirt, a pair of leather boots and a navy Chanel skirt. She says: 'I love trading clothes with friends and it's a great way to get new looks while off-loading stuff you're bored of. I love the environmental side of it; nothing is wasted.'

Drew Barrymore

Drew is the ambassador against hunger for the World Food Programme, along with fellow actress Rachel Weisz. She recently returned from Kenya and is planning a trip to Darfur. She says, 'I can't think of any issue that is more important than working to see that no schoolchild in this world goes hungry. Feeding a child at school is such a simple thing – but it works miracles. I've seen it with my own eyes.'

Julia Roberts

Her Malibu home is environmentally sound, with recycled tiles and bamboo flooring, and she scores top points for recycling her baby clothes (and presumably some of her own) and buying her toddler twins' rompers from charity shops. Roberts supports UNICEF and in 2006 became chairman of Earth Biofuels Advisory Board promoting biodiesel and ethanol.

Angela Lindvall

The American model and actress is a committed environmentalist and vegetarian, and founder and president of the Collage Foundation, which promotes environmentally conscious choices among young people. She was named Best Dressed Environmentalist in 2004 and 2005 by the Seattle-based Sustainable Foundation.

Green Glamour

So now you know who to hang out with in Hollywood, but where does a girl go if she has a red carpet to walk down, or a premier to attend? Those paparazzi flashbulbs can be very unforgiving.

Of course haute couture is an attractive option – the higher up the fashion chain you go, the more sustainable the garment. A Valentino evening gown will be made using only the best-quality, hand-woven fabrics, stitched together by the most highly skilled – and highly paid – seamstresses. Chances are, even the beading, which will probably have been done in India, will be by skilled craftspeople who are well paid and well looked after. Real radicals might indulge in a little recycled haute couture, courtesy of British designer **Gary Harvey**. His fabulous Newspaper Dress, illustrated on the chapter opener, was made using thirty copies of the *Financial Times* and would be guaranteed to make the front page.

There are also a host of hot new designers who are making fabulous clothes from organic materials, using earth-friendly dyeing techniques, and radical new business practice.

In LA, the name to know is **Linda Loudermilk**. At the forefront of eco chic, she uses the most amazing fabrics from recycled tree- and algae-based fibres to reclaimed antique lace, organic cottons and silky bamboo. Or as one of her celebrity fans, Jane Fonda, put it on *The David Letterman Show*: 'It's eco-friendly [fashion]. The top is made of milk and the pants are made of hemp. So you can drink my top and smoke my bottom.' Delicious!

In Europe, there is **Noir**, a 'clean sourcing', designer label founded by the Danish-based Peter Ingwersen. Peter works at the luxury end of the market and has a very loyal following, with celebrities, supermodels and Harvey Nichols customers alike. Making socially responsible fashion sexy, he runs an organic cotton farm in Uganda, which is quite an undertaking – having researched the best seeds to grow in southern Sudan, he then had to seek permission from the UN to use seeds from a war zone!

Noir believes in investing in the future. Their cotton will not be cheap but, if all goes well, Peter will be able to produce enough to use for his own collection, and to sell on to other upmarket fashion houses, keen to buy into the rarefied world of deluxe organic. A percentage of profits will go to the Noir Foundation, which gives back to the African farmers where they need it most. And those who can afford his designs can afford to feel good about themselves too.

Top of any eco A-lister's shopping list, of course, is **Stella McCartney** – beloved by best friends Kate, Gwyneth, Madonna and Natalie Portman, and lusted after by the rest of us.

'We've always worked with organic cotton and denim,' Stella tells me. 'We use organic textiles, bamboo and recycled materials where possible. We're not perfect, and we're not an eco warrior brand, but we are certainly considerate – our business is run on wind power and we use biodegradable corn bags. To think responsibly is rare in the fashion world. But we are not angels and I don't want to be preachy or get on my high horse about it. You can never be perfect – there are always holes to be picked. However, I think a little bit is better than nothing.'

Laura Bailey's guide to wearing green on the red carpet

For big events like Cannes, I mostly wear vintage. I have quite an eccentric mix in my closets: treasures from Rellik and the Hammersmith Fair alongside Oxfam bargains. I don't overthink red carpet dressing. It usually depends on my mood last minute. I also don't care about wearing things again and again – I hate the idea of a one-night-stand dress.

I love Noir and Edun for day or night, and vintage does solve the problem of dressing ethically for the evening, though I am far from perfect. I admire Stella McCartney for both her style and her ethics – a rare example of lack of compromise on any front – and I wear her stuff a lot. As a fellow long-time vegetarian, I especially admire her leather-free shoes and accessories.

Shalom Harlow's tips on eco style

 For red carpet glamour in LA, vintage is a great option. I get a lot of my stuff from Resurrection in Little Italy in New York. I often mix pieces – vintage with organic. It is still a bit challenging to be head-to-toe green for an event-related thing. Fortunately, those red carpet dresses are often borrowed – so in one sense, it is kinda sustainable!

For stylish separates in Hollywood, I'd recommend Anna Cohen (www.annacohen.com), Ecoganik (www.ecoganik.com) and Linda Loudermilk (www.lindaloudermilk.com). Preloved is a fun collection of reworked clothing, made in Toronto, Canada (www.preloved.ca) and Passenger Pigeon – also designed and manufactured in Toronto, offers great pieces and custom-printed fabrics (www.passengerpigeon.ca). Prairie Underground is a super-cute line out of Seattle, and offers some dynamite eco must-haves (www.prairieunderground.com). If you're looking for fine tailoring and extremely good design, try Covet, which is fast becoming 100 per cent eco friendly (www.covetthis.com).

Incidentally, red carpets are about as environmentally unsound as it gets. The red carpet at Cannes – almost 5000 square feet of it – is a typical example. Like most red carpets, it's made of plastic and gets ripped up as soon as the event is over. Perhaps they should start to consider sisal. Or grass.

For Your Own Hollywood Moments
The thinking girl's guide to fur

We all have times when a little Hollywood glamour is called for. And one of the quickest ways to get it is to throw on a fur coat and don some oversized dark sunglasses. But is fur fair (even if it's vintage)? And what are the ethics of faking it?

I remember buying a 1950s fake leopard-print coat when I was about seventeen and feeling like a movie star. These days, the art of glamour doesn't seem so simple. I work in an industry where fur is constantly being promoted. I go to designers' showrooms and have it thrust in front of me, being encouraged to touch it, to witness how soft it feels. I've even been invited to try on the odd mink. All of this makes me feel very uncomfortable. I don't carry a tin of red paint around, of course, and I have to acknowledge that this is a business and if a designer wants to use fur, it's up to them. But watching it slinking down the catwalk does make me feel complicit in the whole thing.

Who's faking it?
Thankfully, not all designers feel the need to visit the chinchilla farm to achieve fluffy glamour. For Paris autumn/winter 2007, Sonia Rykiel used Mongolian lambswool for her multi-coloured finale of 'fur', and Stella McCartney used synthetic material to create the luxury effect for her coats. Giorgio Armani used feathers in place of fur for his Armani Privé haute couture collection for autumn/winter '07. Even Miuccia Prada turned her back on fur (albeit temporarily) with her Fake Classic collection. She claims she was bored with the real thing because it was everywhere. Prada used alpaca and high-tech wool fusions to create fluffy textures that resembled astrakhan and fur.

Of course fur is still everywhere, from Moscow to Milan to the French capital. Everyone from the ladies who lunch to the posers

in the underground clubs are sporting a skinful.
One particular vintage shop in the Marais had
dedicated a whole wall to fox stoles 'plus la tête'. A
personal moral quandary set in when faced with a
1950s cropped fluff-ball of a jacket for only ten euros . . . Surely
the Marilyn effect is OK if it wasn't killed for you? Surely you are
just saving the fifty-year-old garment from decomposing in a
landfill, and setting off harmful methane straight to the ozone
layer? As I say, a true ethical dilemma.

Thankfully, the same shop had a faux-fur version practically
identical. All right, minus the satin pink lining and five euros
more. But still, do I want even to aspire to hang a dead fox (even
a toy one) round my neck? If you feel you can carry off a fake, La
Maison de la Fausse Fourrure in Paris makes fake fur fabrics that
are as soft and as huggable as your childhood cuddly toys. You can
buy imitation wolf or zebra print for around 130 euros per metre
and they look astonishingly real.

There is an argument that fake fur, made from
polyester and other synthetic materials, is harmful to
the environment. According to Global Action
Network, a typical full-length fake fur coat contains at
most 1.3 kilos of synthetics, which translates into the
same energy as five litres of petrol. But in energy
terms, trapped fur costs over 3.5 times as much as
fake fur, and ranched fur costs over fifteen times as
much as fake fur. It is one of those ethical dilemmas
that goes round and round to the point that perhaps
the best option is simply to wear neither.

Ultimately, fur is all about your personal ethics. Jennifer Lopez has no qualms about wearing chinchilla, fox, mink, or pretty much anything with four legs; Naomi Campbell insisted she'd rather go naked than wear fur, before wearing it at every possible occasion; Katharine Hamnett happily wears fake, and somehow makes the look subversive; the latest Peta girl, Rubbish singer Shirley Manson, has worn fake fur but is brilliantly outspoken against the real thing. Chrissie Hynde and daughter Taupe campaign against both real and fake fur.

Look hot in your own skin
By Taupe Hynde, model

We are all style magpies: we absorb striking images and incorporate them, either wholesale or in part, into our own style statements. If you are out and about looking good in your fur trim or vintage fur get-up then others are bound to pick up on what you're wearing. This is how trends are set.

If you wear fur then you should be aware of the facts of the fur trade; in short, you should know how the animal you're wearing lived and died, and how its skin arrived in your clothing.

You should acquaint yourself with the realities of fur production. Manufacturers do not stipulate that their suppliers employ humane methods and so there is no guarantee that slaughterers will wait until the animal is dead before removing its skin.

People who wear vintage fur sometimes say that cruelty is not an issue. I disagree. Today's newly culled hides are the vintage garments of the future – when the animals were tortured and killed is irrelevant. The wearing of any fur, whether ancient or modern, conveys a message that cruelty is fine just so long as it looks good, and this message encourages and promotes the present-day trade.

The buck stops with us: if we are to reject society's apathetic acceptance of cruelty, then we must reject fur's place in fashion. Fur coats are for animals, not for people. Animals' lives are for them, not for us.

Plastic People

While celebrities can give a movement momentum and the cool factor, they are also, of course, capable of doing a whole lot of damage. There's a new breed of celebrities – Paris Hilton, Lyndsay Lohan and Nicole Ritchie spring to mind – who revel in conspicuous over-consumption. Too many handbags, too many clothes, too many belts, too much hair product, too much tan, too many shoes (not enough knickers maybe), it's all too much.

If there is a trend, the plastic people will wear it for all of ten seconds before moving on. Paris even did 'Foho' recently – the new Boho is a more understated, subtle, homespun version of Sienna Miller's hippy deluxe look that spawned a million copycats. It's much more folky (hence the name) and is the perfect vehicle for a bit of hemp, some recycled patchwork smocks, and a chance to revisit your mother's old wardrobe. In other words, it's really not about consuming more clothes and accessories. It's about using what you already have and not buying the designer version off the peg. But for Paris, it's just another fashion trend – here today, gone tomorrow. It's as superficial as that.

Cheap vs chic celebrity style

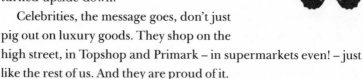

There was a time when celebrities stuck to the ivory-towered fashion houses, and never ventured into the likes of Miss Selfridge or Monsoon. These days Colleen models for George at Asda, and Drew Barrymore poses for New Look, and the whole hierarchy of fashion retailing has turned upside down.

Celebrities, the message goes, don't just pig out on luxury goods. They shop on the high street, in Topshop and Primark – in supermarkets even! – just like the rest of us. And they are proud of it.

It's a very democratic message of course, but it's just adding to the culture in which it has become cool to buy lots and lots of really cheap clothes. If you are struggling to make ends meet, then shop where you can. But if you are a footballer's wife, boasting about your latest buy from Florence & Fred isn't clever. Chances are, you will only wear it once anyway. In fact, that's the way the label is promoted in the UK – the label's TV advertisement shows a girl on horseback getting her dress muddy and then discarding it at the end of her ride. She has another brand new one in her bag. After all, it's just so cheap!

Celebrity couture clash

HOT	**NOT**
Marlene Dietrich for Dior	Melanie Sykes for Matalan
Audrey Hepburn for Givenchy	Drew Barrymore for New Look
Scarlett Johansson for Louis Vuitton	Colleen for George at Asda
William Eggleston & Charlotte Rampling for Marc Jacobs	Tess Daly & Vernon Kay for Tesco

The style makers

As Yves Saint Laurent put it, 'fashions fade, style is eternal'. By its very nature, fashion is unsustainable. Style, on the other hand, is something that evolves as you do. If you need a helping hand finding your look, there are certain designers whose clothes never go out of fashion. Each season simply evolves effortlessly into the next. If you are going to invest in a designer piece, go for style over novelty. Try:

* Giorgio Armani
* Martin Margiela
* Comme des Garçons
* Dries Van Noten
* Ann Demeuelemeester
* Donna Karan
* Yohji Yamamoto

Essentially though, designer names will only get you so far. Style is not something you can go into a shop and buy, or order at the click of a mouse. It's something you have to cultivate as you go along. It's about having a certain way with clothes. It's not about being thin, or tall, hanging out with the right people, or having lots of money. Kate Moss has it. Lily Cole certainly has it. Katharine Hepburn had it. And you can have it too. Just don't go copying anyone else's style.

The fashion clones

The 'as seen on screen' look should be anathema to the green goddess. Unfortunately, on the high street, copycat fashion is all the rage.

Of course we all think that Kate Moss looks cool. She always has done and, I'm sure, she always will. She's Kate Moss, that's why. She could wear a hessian sack and still look the business. But just because she leads a non-stop, alcohol-and-fag-fuelled rock 'n' roll lifestyle, it doesn't mean that such carryings-on would suit the rest of us. It all looks a bit too exhausting to me, guaranteed to give you a hangover and bad skin. Similarly, wearing the clothes she has designed does not mean you'll walk away with her effortless chic. You'll just end up looking like all the other Kate wannabes fighting through the mud at Glastonbury in your thigh high boots, mini-shorts, and 'Glastonbury bag'.

Simply put, wearing the latest celebrity wardrobe to have been translated into a collection for the high street is a big mistake. Chances are, you won't look anything like Madonna, Lily Allen or Scarlett. And even though Kylie's beachwear collection for H&M contributes 10 per cent towards WaterAid, a Kylie bikini should not be bought in the vain belief that it will give you a Kylie bottom.

We need to stop this dressing by numbers. It's like admitting that you don't have a personality or a style or taste of your own. And you know, that's simply not true.

How to Shine Like a Star

* Why copy someone else's style when you can have your own? Explore your own personality and feel free to express yourself in the way you dress. Forget trying to 'get the look'. Try to get your own look instead.
* First of all, take a long hard look in the mirror. What are your best assets? If you have a fabulous figure, show it off and make the most of it. Plunge those necklines, cinch that waist.
* Long legs? Yep, you can wear short skirts, or long skirts, high heels, flat sandals, or pretty much anything you like.
* Short legs? Make sure your clothes are in proportion to you. The current trend for high-waisted jeans might have been made for you. You may want to add a heel.
* Steal from the past, just as the designers do. If you love 1950s Hollywood divas, then bring on the red lipstick. If 1940s austerity is your thing, then look out for Utility label clothes in vintage shops, and practise drawing your seams on your legs.
* You can make the most of your worst asset too. If you hate your hair, or you think your nose is too big, why not make a hat your trademark?
* If you love colour, pile it on. If green is your favourite shade, then make it your signature, from your shoes to your earrings.
* If you like frills, indulge in them to your heart's content.
* If you prefer something a little more masculine, adopt – and adapt – men's suits and make them your own.
* If you love jewellery, pile it on.
* Experiment with your look, and you will soon find your own style which means you don't have to slavishly follow anyone else's.

6

How to Paint the Town Green

How to Paint the Town Green

'Dance till the stars come down from the rafters, Dance, Dance, Dance till you drop'   W. H. Auden

Ethical living wouldn't really be living if it didn't involve living it up, and partying in style. Which is why this chapter is dedicated to good girls and some seriously wicked nights out . . . First up, getting ready:

The Ethical Makeover

Some of us are happy with the looks Mother Nature has blessed us with (or better yet, with the beauty that shines from within). For most of us, however, a little help in the looks department is much appreciated. And these days, that's just fine. Getting dolled up doesn't need to involve industrial quantities of chemicals and enough hairspray to finish off the ozone layer – take note, Jordan! There has been a real explosion recently in organic hair, skin and beauty ranges using natural ingredients that are literally good enough to eat, like soy, rice, pomegranate and cucumber.

If you're the kind of girl who likes her makeup expensive and sleekly packaged, you should try **Stella McCartney's Care** range (produced by YSL Beauté). It's the first mainstream, luxury collection to be organic, and it's guaranteed to make you feel fabulous. For wonderful moisturisers and cleansers, there's plenty on offer from the smaller independent companies who are really setting the standards for the rest of the industry. Top of my list would be the Cornish organic company **Trevarno**, with its simple packaging, pure product and integrity. Pai Skincare, Pangea Organics and Just Pure are also highly recommended for creams and unctions. Try Organic Pharmacy, Origins and Jane Iredale for everything from lip plumpers to carrot butter cleansers. And for glosses and eye pencils, the German firm **Dr Hauschka** is hard to beat. They even do a small range of vegan brushes.

If you are worried about the ingredients in any of your favourite cosmetics or creams, try looking them up on the Environmental Working Group's Skin Deep website: www.cosmeticsdatabase.com. Another useful site is www.theorganicmakeupcompany.com, which has a clearly laid-out glossary explaining everything from aluminium to xanthan gum. The *Ecologist* also works tirelessly at exposing the potentially harmful ingredients we put on our skin in its must-read monthly column, 'Behind the Label'.

Gorgeous pouts and compostable lipstick

Lipstick is one of those instant fixes. If you are feeling a little drab or dowdy, a spot of bright colour or a dab of gloss can work wonders – even if it's the only makeup you have on. It's a treat for your lips, which is why it is so important that it's as pure and natural as you are!

Green People's Organic Red Shimmer Lipstick is a great pick-me-up, proving that organic lipstick does not mean organic sludgy colours.

Cargo's PlantLove Botanical Lipstick is part of a new wave of cosmetics that are fun, fabulous and free from petroleums, parabens and other nasties that you wouldn't dream of putting on your face (though many of us do, all of the time). It's amazing how excited you can get over a tube of lipstick – especially when you discover that the packaging is made from corn and can be chucked on your compost heap when you've finished with it. The outer paper packing is pressed with seeds and will actually grow when you plant it, and the lipstick itself is as red and shiny as they come.

Aveda is one of the biggest, eco-beauty brands on the market. It leads the way in using organic, natural ingredients, recycled and refillable packaging, and policies that support cultural and ecological diversity. More to the point, Aveda also boasts some gorgeous products: check out the Environmetal Compacts, and the Uruku Lip Pigments: lipsticks that boast rich, conditioning colour and a red seed-pigment straight from the Urukum palm (grown by Brazil's Yawanawa tribe).

Powder puffs

One of the worst things about cosmetics, and also the reason why they are so fabulously seductive, is the amount of unnecessary packaging they use. You can get around this by using a lovely old powder compact, simply refilling as you go from a big pot of loose powder. Not only will you look ultra glamorous as you peer into your mirror, you also save throwing away a perfectly good plastic compact every time you run out of powder. Natural cosmetics company **Lavera** does a great organic powder – you can buy it from the organic apothecary www.lovelula.com.

Paint the town – and your nails – red

Do you love nail varnish but hate the fact that it smells so toxic? I've begun to feel allergic to the smell of it, and was thrilled to find that there is an alternative.

For nail varnish that is toluene- and formaldehyde-free, try the German company **Sante**. The natural and organic skincare website www.theremustbeabetterway.com stocks the range. I recommend the Shiny Red (for toes), and the acetate-free nail varnish remover, made with organic ethanol, once you're done. Remember, you can always take your own varnish and remover with you when you go for a manicure or pedicure – it might encourage your salon to go organic too.

Why organic matters
By Stella McCartney, designer

I always wanted to use organic skin care, but it had really bad textures, smelt awful and the packaging was usually so unattractive, I would end up being seduced by all the conventional stuff, even though it's full of silicone. I wanted to know, if we ditch the silicone will it feel lumpy?

Your skin is your largest organ and absorbs up to 60 per cent of what you put on it. This means that over your lifetime, you absorb two kilograms of chemicals from conventional beauty products. And lots of skin products use the same petrochemicals as the antifreeze in your car!

At the high end of the industry I'm in, the word organic is underused. Asking YSL Beauté to develop an organic skincare range was a real challenge. In fact, it has taken over three years to develop the Care range. But the brand really knows about luxury and when you take that and apply it to organic you can make something really special. It's quite rewarding to see how my friends react now, when I give it them to try. They expect the products to be a bit funky and treehuggy, and they're surprised. Hopefully it means organics are here to stay rather than being a passing trend.

I'm not interested in preaching. I just want to try and give people information. When I started with the range I wanted to know why organic was better, or in fact even if it was better for you. I didn't know. But I have since found that the active ingredients in raw organic materials far outweigh conventional ones, sprayed with pesticides. When a plant has been sprayed with chemicals, it means its own immune system isn't working.

When I had my first baby, I looked at him and thought what do you put on skin that is so pure and vulnerable? I couldn't use anything that I had already. In the end, I resorted to organic olive oil. And then you start to think, at what age do you start to put any old crap on your skin? It's so important to be aware and be informed. 〝

How to make your own face pack

There's nothing better than a gorgeous, gunky facemask to prepare you for a big night out. Here's the perfect recipe to make you glow:

* First prepare a sage infusion. For this you'll need a small handful of sage leaves infused in a pint of boiling water.
* Leave to cool.
* Beat one egg white.
* Apply to face with sponge.
* Allow to dry and repeat.
* When thoroughly dry, apply beaten yoke.
* Lie and rest for at LEAST half an hour.
* Rinse with warm water.
* Pat on sage leaf infusion.

Home treatments for your hair
By Peter Gray, hairdresser to the stars

❝❝   Are there really any good natural, organic ways of maintaining a healthy barnet? The answer is as subjective as finding a facial moisturiser (natural or otherwise) that suits and works for each and every individual. Whether you have bleached blonde hair, naturally wavy locks or afro curls, the principle for looking after your hair is the same: hair is an appendage to the skin. Cleansing and conditioning regularly with a pH-neutral, non-detergent-based product will keep your hair in tiptop condition. With the fashion for shiny hair it's difficult to achieve this naturally, as hair that is not clean does not reflect light.

As for colouring, there is no such a thing as a natural way to colour hair, but there are ways of minimising damage both to your scalp and the environment. Look out for the vegetable dye content or components in all colourings, and avoid metallic dyes. I've worked a lot with Aveda and I'm a big fan of Cowshed. I would also recommend Phyto, Kiehls, Nude and Eufora. Alternatively, raid your kitchen for some natural hair treatments:

* Lemon juice (and vodka), plus sun, definitely lightens blonde hair. Apply when hair is damp rather than wet.
* Raw eggs, especially the yolks, are a source of concentrated protein, as is mayonnaise.
* A cider vinegar rinse in a spritzer bottle is alkali and will close and smooth the cuticles, resulting in a shinier surface.
* Try tomato ketchup on reds, carrot juice on gingers and chamomile tea on blondes.
* Green tea will minimise unwanted warm tones in blondes.
* Beer is supposed to have conditioning properties but it seems an awful waste.

Recipes for beautiful hair

Natural hairspray

Fresh fruit:
½ orange
½ lemon

Chop fruit into small pieces in a pot with two cups of boiling water. Boil until liquid reduces by half. Cool, strain and place in spray bottle. Store in refrigerator or add one ounce of rubbing alcohol to store at room temperature for up to two weeks. Add water to reduce stickiness, if desired.

Frizz control

1 small aloe vera leaf

Slice leaf and squeeze gel into palm. Massage into hair.

Red hair enhancer

½ cup beetroot juice
½ cup carrot juice

Pour over clean damp hair. Wrap with plastic and wrap hot towel on top. Sit under medium dryer heat or sit in sun for one hour. Shampoo.

Brunette hair dye

Triple-strength black coffee

Rinse damp hair with coffee repeatedly using the coffee several times. Leave on for fifteen minutes. Rinse with clear water.

Chamomile brightener for blonde hair

> *6 chamomile tea bags*
> *½ cup of plain yogurt*
> *7 drops of lavender oil*

Steep tea bags for fifteen minutes. Combine yogurt and lavender oil with tea. Mix thoroughly. Apply to hair and leave for thirty minutes with hair wrapped in cap. Shampoo.

Dry hair

> *1 banana*
> *1 egg*
> *¼ cup honey*
> *3 tablespoons of milk*
> *5 tablespoons olive oil*

Massage into scalp and then hair. Set for fifteen minutes. Shampoo.

Avocado deep conditioner

> *1 small jar of mayonnaise*
> *½ an avocado*

Mix together and apply to hair for twenty minutes. Shampoo.

All Dressed Up . . .

So you've got your face on, your hair is immaculate (as long as you remembered to rinse off all that egg yolk and ketchup!), and you're ready to party. But what to do for fun? Thankfully, now that you're part of the ethical elite, there's no end of brilliant nights to be had. And these are nights to stretch your imagination. No more sitting, bored out of your brain, in some corporate chain-pub. No more being packed like sardines in line at the latest Superclub. It's time to get fresh, and go wild . . .

The great swap shop

The biggest trend to hit fashionland this year is the swishing party. Embraced by the likes of Mischa Barton, Sadie Frost and Thandie Newton, the basic idea is that you take a couple of pieces of clothing that are too good to give to charity but that you've stopped wearing, and you come home with somebody else's fabulous cast-offs.

Like fashion itself, swishing is thoroughly international and everyone has their own way of swapping items. At a recent club night put on by the arty London collective Wowwow! the cloakroom was turned into a fashion exchange for the night. It was less of a swap and more of a lucky dip. One club-goer gave in a worn-out jacket and gained a fetching Prada waistcoat on her way out. Another, due to alcohol-induced enthusiasm, gave up his whole outfit, and got mostly girls' clothes in return.

In America, swishing is a more organised, regulated affair. Professional companies will arrange your party for you. American 'Swap-O-Rama-Rama' will not only organise a swap, but will hold workshops afterwards where you can sew your newfound clothes into recycled pieces, or just tailor them to you. They even supply new labels with the words '100% Recycled' or 'Recycled by Me' to cover up the old labels. At the end of the session, they have a fun catwalk to show off the creations. Swap-O-Rama-Rama even has its own philosophy: 'Through hands-on experience, Swap-O-Rama-Rama invites the discovery that the making of things is not an activity to be avoided in order to attain leisure, but rather a playful and leisurely endeavor unto itself.' It's as much about the social experience as the final result of finding yourself a lovely new outfit.

Another American company that takes swishing to a more sophisticated level, with themed nights like the 'Devil swaps Prada', 'Swapping for vintage fans' and 'Swapping for foodies' is www.clothingswap.org.

In the UK, we have our own online swap shop, www.whats mineisyours.com, set up by fashion expert Judy Berger. As well as buying and selling, the site has a swapping page. And Swap-A-Rama Razzmatazz is a clothes swap night with a difference: instead of bringing clothes and swapping you arrive in an outfit you no longer want and every time the klaxon sounds each reveller swaps one item they are wearing, until you have a full new outfit. The usual venue is east London's Favella Chic club.

It's the social interaction that makes swishing so much fun – and gives you as much of a thrill as a spending spree at the shops. The Feather Duster 'swap 'til you drop' parties, hosted by the ethical events organisers Hybird, are held at a pub and feature cupcakes and a customisation station (where two girls with sewing machines are on hand to alter your new finds or even stitch two of them together). Any leftover clothes are donated to Traid.

Swishing parties can be hysterical affairs – especially if there is alcohol involved. As soon as the swish is declared open, it's elbows out and the fun begins. At one Futerra party, a Chloé Paddington was fiercely fought over, but it's not just designer labels that are the objects of desire. You never know what will catch someone's eye – and possibly become their most treasured item. (Until they get bored with it of course, and decide it's time to swap it on . . .)

Names to remember
www.futerra.co.uk
www.swaporamarama.org
www.whatsmineisyours.com
www.clothingswap.org
www.myspace.com/hybirdproductions

How to swap clothes without losing friends

If you are feeling brave, host your own swishing party. All you need are: a few friends, a rail if you have one – it helps add to the frisson if the clothes are hanging on a rail like in a shop – and your best cast-offs. You might want to cover the pile of clothes with a sheet before starting. Blow a whistle and let the mayhem ensue.

* It's a nice idea to provide Fairtrade wine and some snacks to get everyone in the mood before the swish begins. It's not a good idea to swish on an empty stomach.
* You have to be a good sport with swishing, as some of your old clothes might end up being the entertainment for the evening; remember, the more dedicated to fashion you are the more likely it is that you will have some 'adventurous' pieces that might be open to a bit of light-hearted ridicule.
* Be confident, especially if you have a long-limbed size-eight friend who can make the bin-bags her clothes came in look good.
* Full-length mirrors are extremely useful – and add to the changing room experience.
* Obviously clean and iron everything and make sure you empty your pockets and bags.
* If there is a fight, flip a coin. Don't go down the 'who does it

look better on' route as you will end up hurting someone.
* Remember, one woman's trash is another woman's treasure. You really won't believe what others don't want.

An A–Z of Good Nights Out (and In)

American Apparel parties
The Old Blue Last is a pub on London's Curtain Road that is the antithesis of the new sterile high street chain-pub. See people like Kate Nash sing there or check out the regular parties hosted by American Apparel and *Vice* magazine. No one quite knows how to get on the guest list, but dressing ethically might help.

Bowling belles
For a great retro night out, put on your bowling shoes and strike! Liberty Ross, Sienna Miller and Leah Wood have all been spotted at the deluxe bowling alley, All Star Lanes (www.allstarlanes.co.uk), in London's Bloomsbury. Not particularly green or ethical, but there is something wonderfully retro and uplifting about a night out at the bowling alley. Plus, we love the shoes.

Creative artists
Wowwow are a south London arts collective that started a few years ago with Matthew Stone, Gareth Pugh and other artists, DJs and bands. Their squat parties have become the stuff of clubland legend and have included clothes swaps and drawing on walls. For the latter, everyone was handed out pens and paints and encouraged to cover the walls in their 'art'.

If you're up in the north of England, check out Mr Scruff, who puts on a monthly day-to-night in the Contact Theatre in Manchester, called Sketch City. Graffiti artists produce pieces of art over the day, and everyone can draw on the tables and walls. See www.myspace.com/sketchcity and www.mrscruff.com.

Dining out

This is one of the most satisfying and easy ways to have an ethical night out. In a way, the new generation of eco-restaurants is an evolution of the health food cafes of the 1970s, but the new breed is altogether more stylish and sophisticated – rest assured you won't find an earthenware bowl of chewy brown rice in sight. It's not just about the food, but the interiors, the water, the recycling processes and the food miles. At the moment, restaurants that take these factors into consideration are a novelty, but it can't be long before such issues are standard practice.

The best is London's first seriously eco-restaurant, Acorn House in King's Cross (www.acornhouserestaurant.com), where all the hard work – the recycling, the water purifying, the transport using biodiesel, the right ingredients, even the bellinis (with seasonal rhubarb) – has been done for you. Inspired!

Dinner parties

A great way to save on your carbon footprint is to stay home and invite some friends over. Don't be tempted by a takeaway. Think of all that packaging! Sustainable eating is where it's at. Make your own pizza and you can even get your friends to join in. Or take some tips from Cocktail Girl, Polly Vernon, and host your own cocktail hour.

* Easy pizza: first, make your bread dough, using organic yeast and flour of course. Roll it out, and add seasonal toppings of your choice, from organic tomato sauce, peppers, olives, onions, mushrooms, artichokes, sardines and mozzarella. Keep it seasonal and, ideally, use the herbs from your window box (basil, rocket, oregano etc.). Bake for ten minutes in a hot oven. Serve with homemade coleslaw. For this you'll need organic cabbage, carrots, a touch of onion and an apple, all thinly sliced

and mixed with mayo, salt and pepper. Throw
in some caraway seeds if you like.

* Shop at your local farmers' market: buy only
  what is in season – preferably local and organic – and
  ask the stallholder for tips on how to cook your ingredients.
  They know all the best ways and will be happy to oblige.
* Ask your guests to bring a dish: there's nothing like asking your
  friends to do their bit to add to the communal spirit. If you
  haven't got time yourself to cook, simply ask everyone to bring
  their favourite food and have a picnic.
* Throw a cake party: a good idea for Sunday afternoons, tell
  your friends to bring a cake (preferably home-baked). You
  supply the organic cream and strawberries.
* Make your own organic ice cream: invest in an ice cream maker
  and all you need is some good cream, sugar, organic seasonal
  fruits and berries. It's really easy, you know exactly what's gone
  into it, and your friends will be impressed.

How to impress your friends without being an eco bore

Dinner party conversation pieces:

The energy we save when we recycle one glass bottle
can run a lightbulb for four hours.

*   *   *

If the sea temperature were to rise by one degree
Centigrade, all the coral reefs would be destroyed.

*   *   *

Female hammerhead sharks have got the right idea –
they have no need for men as they have adapted to
reproduce asexually. No one realised they could do this

until 2001 when a baby shark appeared in a tank of three females. Come on girls, if they can do it . . .

*   *   *

There are only fifty years of fish stocks left if we continue to fish at the present level.

*   *   *

In the Amazon, an area the size of Wales is cut down every year.

*   *   *

Thirty per cent of the world's land surface is covered in forest. If this were shared out equally it would amount to an area the size of a football pitch for each person.

*   *   *

A third of male fish in English rivers are changing sex due to 'gender-bending' pollution – experts say female hormones from the contraceptive pill and HRT are being washed into our rivers and causing males to produce eggs.

*   *   *

More is known about the moon than the ocean, which covers 71 per cent of our earth.

*   *   *

One cupful of pesticides and fertilisers is used in the production of a typical non-organic T-shirt, and up to a third of the weight of that T-shirt is made up from chemical residues.

How to mix ethics and cocktails
By Polly 'Cocktail Girl' Vernon

66 Ethics and cocktails is a much stickier issue than I first imagined. According to my cocktail sources – the various bar owners, consultants and bartenders who know anything about it at all, and who, furthermore, were prepared to talk about it – ethical issues can't really be applied to cocktails. This is partly because the production of spirits is fundamentally unregulated – many liquors are produced in tiny, far-flung parts of the world, on one small hacienda in Mexico for example, or some remote part of the Caribbean, and they're made according to obscure traditional methods which have been passed down through generations of artisans. And after one Tequila Sunrise, who cares any more, anyway?

It is possible, however, to have guilt-free cocktails if you make your own. Here are a few tips:

* Do make sure your rum is fair trade. You can buy Fairtrade white rum from supermarkets and look out too for Utkins, a Fairtrade and organic spirits label that supports 800 sugar cane farmers in Paraguay. They make organic vodka too.
* Do drink bourbon or Scotch whisky to your heart's content. It's produced by employees protected by unions; there are even reforestation policies on the barrels.
* Don't add out-of-season fruit to your cocktails. Try to buy local organic berries and citrus fruit that haven't been flown across the world.
* Don't put too much plastic paraphernalia in your drinks. Keep the umbrellas and pink flamingoes down to a minimum.
* Do use Fairtrade and organic coconut milk.
* Do make sure your glasses are recycled. You can get a decent set

of recycled hi-ball glasses from www.ecotopia.co.uk.

* Do grow your own organic mint, perfect for whipping up an impromptu mint julep or mojito.

A really green mint julep

6 parts bourbon
1 tbsp Fairtrade sugar syrup
10–15 mint leaves

Mix the mint leaves and sugar syrup in a chilled hi-ball glass. Fill with crushed ice and add bourbon, and pretend you are somewhere exotic.

Eco clubbing

Sound Impact is Manchester's first one hundred per cent eco club night. Run by Action for Sustainable Living and Manchester Student Union, the night involves drinks from local, organic and ethical suppliers, carbon-offsetting and even a low-impact promotional campaign. For more details, see www.afsl.org.uk. Look out for more, or start your own.

Folky nights out

The Queens of Noize have a regular 'folking it up' night. This is folk meets space age (they dress up in gold and silver foil, which we are sure they recycle afterwards). Glam folk rock, if you can imagine such a thing. Playlists include songs with such titles as 'Emerald Forest' and 'Willow Tree', so there's an eco sentiment there somewhere. See www.myspace.com/queensofnoize.

Green house

All partied out? If you're too tired to go out, or reluctant to get your ethically-aware butt out of the house, why not stay in and clean up? Stay clear of chemical cleaners and make sure your washing-up liquid, surface cleaner, bath and loo scourers are all biodegradable and easy on the planet. Ecover, Bio-D and Clearspring are all good (who cares about a bit of limescale in your toilet?). In fact, as every domestic green goddess knows, all you really need to clean your home are a few lemons, a bottle of vinegar, some baking powder – and a lot of elbow grease.

Karaoke

Nothing can be more uplifting than a good karaoke session. Hire a booth with some friends, select your favourite songs, and sing until you are hoarse. If you are really serious, you can take along your own instruments – or even dress up as your favourite star.

Mailing lists

Join Anti-Apathy's mailing list and get invited to one of their lively discussion nights. Or sign up to Beyond Retro's list and get yourself invited to shop-and-roll evening events at Christmas and Valentine's Day, complete with refreshments and bands. See the Little Green Book, at the back, for more details.

In case you hadn't realised, we are in the middle of a 1980s revival, which threatens to turn into a 1990s revival at any minute. With its neon bright colours and streak of total hedonism, you may wonder what our green goddess is doing dressing up in – I can barely write the words – a *shell suit*. But Nu Rave harks back to the acid house summer of love. It's all about the DIY ethic we love, and a revolt against consumerism and the corporate heads that run the creative businesses. It's for fashion designers, musicians and club promoters who are fed up with not being heard, and are doing it for themselves. So of course a guide to great nights would be incomplete without mentioning the ultimate party high.

Nu rave: A beginner's guide
By Namalee Bolle of Super Super *magazine*

Clothes are not about the label or how expensive they are; everything has a function. My style is 'tramp like'; it's 'maxi-maxi-maximalism'. I wear bathing suits and leggings for performing on stage. The clubbing and music scene is fast-paced. Sports clothes enable you to move. I wear trainers because they are utilitarian so I am close to the ground, and my physicality is not altered by the falseness of heels.

Jewellery is big. 'Neck-breakers' are large chains with anything you can find hanging off them: abacuses represent money, clocks represent the passing of time. My clothes are very warrior like, everything is on the outside.

The fashion is about sharing: dressing is not a competition, it's a collective effort – making jewellery for a friend or finding something and realising it looks better on someone else. Clothes are from charity shops, as well as found objects, disco balls, and toys. My ethic plays with the value of greed.

Objects and clothes are old and rescued, nothing matches, nothing goes to waste, everything means something but the value is personal and not material.

I like to be 'an assault on the eyes' – it's about playing with the rules and not being a slave to seasonal trends. I want people to have a giggle when they see me on the tube. At least it's a reaction.

My heroes are Sponge Bob Square Pants, Timmy Mallet and Eddie the Eagle.

A nu-rave shopping list:

Trucker caps

Gilets

Big baggy trousers (Sporty Spice style but it works!)

Leggings

Shell suits

Bathing suits

Bikinis

Anything UV or day-glo

Tie-dye but rave style

Leg warmers

High-top trainers, preferably white or pink

Sunglasses, bigger the better

National Health Jarvis glasses

Gold jewellery

Roller disco

Dressing up is encouraged at the weekly roller disco in Vauxhall in south London. Like bowling, there is something fabulously retro about a roller disco. Look out for old rollerblades at charity shops, pretend you're a waitress in a 1950s diner, and off you spin (see www.rollerdisco.info).

Swing

The Rakehells Revels has become an institution every Tuesday night at the decadent Grill Room at Café Royal. It's the perfect place to wear your best vintage 1920s and 1940s clothes, and dance to a mix of swing, jazz and rhythm 'n' blues. Check out www.rakehells.com.

Take part in a record auction

These take place sporadically and you have to be in the know, but they are a great way of meeting friends, having a few drinks, having a dance, buying a record you've always wanted and giving to charity! If you can't wait to be invited to one, why not arrange your own? Basically, eight DJs play for half an hour each using records bought from charity shops – for under £10. A pound on the door goes to charity and you can 'bid' on a record you like when you hear it. The highest bidder wins . . . And, of course, proceeds go to the charity of the organiser's choice.

Vague nights out

Born out of the Glastonbury Festival, Lost Vagueness is part circus, part cabaret, part casino, part chaos, with a good dose of old-style music hall thrown in. Join the madness in the Lost Vagueness Field at Glastonbury, or see them at a venue near you. You can join in too. They are always on the look-out for costumes: evening wear, military, western, Victorian, retro, accessories – you name it. Sounds like they need to set up a swishing party (see www.lostvagueness.com).

7

Great
Escapes

Great Escapes

'Airplane travel is nature's way of making you look like your
passport'
                                                          Al Gore

How to Travel Light

Holidays are a chance to escape – to put your worries aside,
reconnect with what's important, or find a fresh perspective
on life. It used to be that jetting off to the other side of the world
was the ultimate dream. And let's face it, when you've only got a
week to soak up the sun and totally unwind, away from work
pressures, a quick, cheap plane trip is incredibly tempting. But
remember, modern airports are hardly the most relaxing of places:
the neon lights, the inevitable delays, the queues to get past
security – it's a rare soul who won't find the experience a little
hellish. And that's not to mention the environmental impact of
flying, which – as we know – is awful.

Plane travel is responsible for about 40 million tonnes of carbon
emissions a year and it's on its way to becoming the single biggest
source of greenhouse gas emissions by 2050. It might be the norm,
but it simply isn't sustainable. So to help you (and me) resist the

temptations of those Easy flights – just a click away! – I've enlisted
some free spirits to guide you through the world of alternative
travel and authentic adventure. Forget sightseeing agendas and
all-inclusive deals, here are trips that won't cost the earth, but will
expand your horizons and enrich your imagination.

Go to the end of this chapter for the last word on carbon
offsetting. First up, though, it's time to get packing . . .

How to pack

Being a fashion assistant does have its positive side, and during my
time spent being suffocated by clothes in various overheated
fashion cupboards around London, I learnt a thing or two about
packing suitcases. Now fashion people are not renowned
for their ability to travel light – just one pair of shoes per
day is quite a compromise – but there is an art to laying
everything out as flat as can be:

* Tuck tissue paper between layers.
* Put your shoes and washbags (make that washbag, singular)
  around the edges.
* Invest in recyclable, reusable miniature plastic containers for
  your shampoos and other unctions so that you don't end up
  dragging a family-sized bottle of shampoo across the world
  unnecessarily. Muji has a great selection.
* Decant a small bottle of Ecover clothes wash so that you can
  pack fewer clothes and wash them as you go.
* If you are going to the beach, all you really need is a bikini
  (unless you are going *au naturale* which is probably the most eco
  way to sunbathe). There is an Italian company that has
  designed a biodegradable one, but I can't vouch for it not
  dissolving as you dive in the sea.
* Take some flip-flops – Patagonia's Shore Things are made from
  cork, leather and recycled nylon, or Worn Again's Car Sandal is

made from recycled car-seat leather and seat belts.

* An organic cotton beach towel from www.greenfibres.co.uk and some kind of sarong – perhaps bought locally – should complete the look.

* If you decide to pack everything into a rucksack, don't forget to use our favourite fabric, hemp (www.thehempshop.co.uk not only sells rucksacks but a suitcase on wheels too).

Don't forget your kikoi

I never travel without my kikoi. These traditional striped cotton scarves were originally made for fishermen in East Africa and come in a range of luscious stripes and colours. I use mine as a sarong on the beach, for lying on, and lying underneath when the sun gets too hot, and when it gets chilly you can use it as a shawl or just as an extra layer. Now, a small British company **Kica & Ferret** is working directly with kikoi makers in Kenya to produce the traditional textiles in cool colours and stripes.

The golden fleece

From a fashion point of view, the fleece is a non-starter of course, but it is a really great example of what Sarah Ratty calls a 'super synthetic'. Incredibly warm, light and useful to have on holiday, the most fabulous point of them is that they can – and should – be made by recycling plastic bottles.

Patagonia started the whole thing in the early 1990s. I remember getting very excited about it at the time, and that was before I fully realised how much of the world's landfill plastic bottles were taking up. Berghaus, Timberland and Howies all now make outdoor clothes using eco fleece. And Marks & Spencer is recycling theirs to make lovely crackly polyester trousers and school uniforms! Apparently it takes just twenty-five bottles to make a medium-sized fleece. It's a shame it doesn't use more because on average, every UK household uses 440 plastic bottles each year, of which just twenty-four – only enough to make one fleece – are recycled.

The best sunscreens

If you want your sunscreen to be organic, and free of synthetic perfumes or petroleum-derived polymers, there are now some really great products on the market. Look for mineral sunblocks (that use titanium or zinc oxide) if you have problems with chemical sunscreens irritating your skin.

Try these:

Green People
Weleda
Dr Hauschka
Aveda
Yaoh
Neal's Yard (they also do a great organic citronella spray
    to keep insects at bay)
Aubrey Organics
Ecolani

●★◉★

Holiday One: Slow Travel –
a Round-the-World Trip . . .

The key to sustainable travel is time. If you've got a year to meander through the world, then of course you can take the slowest – and often the cheapest – route, and enjoy the journey as much as the destination. Take inspiration from Ed Gillespie, founder of the sustainable communications company Futerra. As I write this, Ed is travelling around the world, without flying, one of the new champions of slow and low-carbon travel.

Rail Experience – the top three train journeys
By Ed Gillespie, slow traveller

1. ***Vienna to Graz, Austria – The Semmeringbahn***
   This spectacular journey, the first railway to be listed under UNESCO World Heritage guidelines, passes through incredible Alpine scenery and over numerous bridges, viaducts and amazing tunnels – simply mind-blowing!

2. ***Circum Baikal Railway, Siberia***
   This is the remnant of a grand railway that once flanked the world's oldest, deepest lake. The six-hour, 90-kilometre, single-track journey is a slow travel classic! It takes you along rugged cliffs and crags and through thirty-eight tunnels above Lake Baikal. In winter the ice below is a perfectly smooth white sheet stretching over to the snow-capped mountains on the far shore; in summer you can see 40 metres down into the clear blue waters. Magical in either season.

3. *Trans-Siberian Railway, Moscow: Irkutsk*

The daddy of slow travel, the Trans-Siberian is probably the only train journey on which you can get jet-lag! The full Moscow to Vladivostok route takes two weeks, passes through seven time zones and, at nearly 9300 km, is the longest continuous railway trip on the planet. Marvel at the rolling landscape, grow to love the view of passing birch trees, sample the culinary delights of Baboushkas on the platforms and of course enjoy a vodka (bottle) or three with your fellow passengers.

Tips for occupying yourself on long journeys:

1. **Explore**: you're free to wander around on trains so make the most of it. Sate your curiosity about the differences between the various classes. Investigate the edibility of the various offerings of the buffet car. Review the loo!
2. **Share**: take snacks, sweets and alcohol to share with your fellow passengers – a great way to spark conversation, and when linguistic abilities are limited it prompts lots of polite smiling and nodding. On some trains, you can even whip out a knife and make sandwiches, which is somewhat unwelcome on planes these days.
3. **Turn on your observation skills**: don't let the scenery hypnotise you! Train travel allows you to get a real feel for the countryside you are passing through, revealing the details of life and culture in a way that's impossible from a plane at 50,000 feet. Whether it's drunken Russians sleeping by the track or Mongolian camel-herding techniques, don't let it pass you by.
4. **The obvious stuff**: take a good book or two and catch up on your reading – a book relevant to your journey will enhance the experience (*Dr Zhivago* made our Trans-Siberian express

journey). Snooze gently to the rhythm of the rails. Playing cards, draughts, chess or drinking games with your travel companions certainly helps to pass the time.

5. **Travel with your lover**: sod the mile-high club – this is better/ easier, however, if you have your own compartment!

Read Ed Gillespie's blog – and perhaps follow in his very faint carbon footsteps – at www.lowcarbontravel.com.

For more, great advice on how to travel by rail or ship, check out 'the man in Seat 61', or rather, his wonderful website: www.seat61. com. One of his best recommendations is to plan your journey with the indispensable world timetables. *The Thomas Cook European Timetable* can be consulted for train, bus and ferry times for every country in Europe, and *The Thomas Cook Overseas Timetable* for every country in the world outside Europe.

If you don't have a year to indulge your spirit of adventure, there are still plenty of ways to enjoy foreign trips. All you need is a bit of planning, and knowing what you fancy:

Holiday Two: Teach the World to Sing

Living proof that eco friendly doesn't have to mean cosy or crusty, our favourite DJ and blonde-haired vixen Sam Hall, aka Goldierocks, spends six months a year trekking from field to field, spreading her eclectic mix of music around the globe.

Attend any of the below and Goldierocks guarantees that you'll
have the most fabulously debauched time, without living off two-
day-old greasy bacon baps and having to treat a mysterious cow-
pat-induced rash when you get home.

Goldierock's guide to festivals

1. **Burning Man Festival** (Nevada Desert, USA). Burning Man is
    the epitome of a self-contained, non-corporate, ethical festival.
    Created, enjoyed and entirely destroyed by participants on an
    annual basis, culminating in the highlight of a burning effigy
    of a wicker man. A warning though, this isn't for the faint
    hearted – in the middle of the Nevada Desert with no 'official'
    organisation, you have to be well prepared or face rather nasty
    consequences. What an adventure though.
2. **The Secret Garden Party** (Cambridge, UK). This well-kept
    secret is a highlight on an eco fashionista's calendar. Tastefully
    intimate but most definitely not lacklustre in line-up. Last year
    it boasted Lily Allen, The Automatic and Graham Coxon as
    headliners – all self-proclaimed nature lovers. OK, I made that
    bit up, but the ethos is most certainly non-corporate, as the
    name suggests. Think secret fairytale garden party over
    glorified mud-endurance test.
3. **Glastonbury** (Glastonbury, UK). The godfather of ethical
    festivals – Glasto boasts long-term backing from Oxfam and
    Greenpeace. The Woodstock of our time.
4. **Exit Festival** (Novi Sad, Serbia). A rising favourite among
    serious festival-goers. Exit was initially a festive offshoot of the
    youth movements that campaigned against strongman leader
    Slobodan Milosevic during the 1990s. The festival now draws
    music lovers to Novi Sad from all over the region's war-scarred
    countries, and it's a great way of generating tourism and
    promoting political awareness. Oh, and with The Beastie
    Boys and Lauryn Hill headlining it has one of the best festival

line-ups in Europe for 2007.

5. **Big Day Out** (various cities, Australia). Conducting its own independent research into the waste generated by the massive touring festival, Big Day Out has voluntarily adopted a carbon-neutral emission footprint for its 2007 show. Very fancy.

6. **Bestival** (Isle of Wight, UK). Growing larger every year, but keeping hold of Rob Da Bank's strong worldwide community ethic. Highlights for the more picky of us who 'don't do' the camping thing include private solar-panelled T-pees (yes that's to fuel the en-suite showers) and a charitable donation to Crisis included in the hire fee.

7. **The Green Man Festival** (Wales, UK). Kooky anti-folk at its very best and no Carling beer tents here, thank you very much. All food and alcohol is from local producers, so that's organic, farm-reared beefburgers and homemade cider all served in recyclable, biodegradable containers.

8. **Sonar** (Barcelona, Spain). As well as hosting world-class live acts and DJs, this progressive arts festival is renowned for putting on a variety of politically challenging performance art, tackling issues such as global warming and child labour.

9. **Earthcore** (Queensland, Australia). One of the most famous dance festivals in Australia, teaching Europe a thing or two about crowd control, taking care of their thousands of drooling ravers by giving out free sunscreen and recyclable water bottles.

10. **Blues & Rock Festival** (Byron Bay, Australia). Hosted on the crystal clean beaches of Byron Bay, homeland to and renowned place of exodus for hippies from all over Down Under.

To check Goldierocks' whereabouts, go to www.goldierocks.co.uk.

Holiday Three: Be a Happy Camper

A camping holiday is one of your greenest options. Just removing the need to fly to your destination means you have a much lower impact on the environment. Add to this the fact that you're not using air conditioning or electricity and much less water (who needs to bath every day?) and you can be assured that you're even more eco friendly than you would be at home.

Kat Heyes, who drew all the beautiful illustrations for this book, is also a passionate camper and, along with her sister-in-law Tess Carr, has just published a book *The Happy Campers* on the subject. Tess and Kat are absolute experts in this field (excuse the pun), so here's their take on the joys of camping holidays.

Camping has recently become the stylish thing to do and what with the boom in new festivals, designer tents and tailor-made yurt holidays there are no signs of that trend abating. We think that it's more than just a passing fad, simply because there are so many things that make a camping holiday fantastic.

Being outdoors every day surrounded by beautiful countryside and breathing in all that fresh air is good for your soul. Away from everyday stresses and the reminders of our increasingly technological world you can really enjoy the simple things in life, the smell of the campfire, running to be first in the sea or just your friends laughing. Camping strips us back to basics and helps us remember what's really precious in our lives.

You also get to enjoy your friends and family when they are at their most natural and relaxed. Camping is great for friendships; pitching in together to 'survive', making your own entertainment, gathering around the campfire after a hard day having fun. It's a very social experience and seems to bond you together much more than any other type of holiday.

Camping is also really cheap and very easy to organise. You can plan ahead for longer trips or be spontaneous and just head off for the weekend with no fixed plan. Whatever happens and wherever you end up it's always guaranteed to be an adventure. 🙰

The happy camper's top five sites of all time

1. **Friendly farms**, various fields on the South Downs
    As we live in Brighton we love just packing up the car and zooming off somewhere nearby for a couple of nights campout. We've approached a few friendly farmers and asked if they have a spare field we could camp in. They have been very generous – some even provide a bit of firewood – and we usually have the whole field to ourselves. It's a great way to have a bit of nature all to yourself. Always ask permission, don't make too much noise and respect their land and livestock.

2. **Henry's Campsite**, Cornwall
    Cornwall is very close to our hearts and we both try and visit there at least once a year. This small, family-run site is the most southerly in Britain. Set amidst beautiful countryside, most pitches have a spectacular sea view. Within walking distance is the next village, Cadgwith, a working fishing village, where boats are pulled up on to the cove shore by tractor and fresh fish is sold for your evening BBQ. The local pub has Cornish singsongs on Fridays, so bring your musical instruments and lubricate your tonsils!

3. **Dales Farm Camping**, Dunfermline
    This eco-friendly campsite has dry composting toilets, a badger hide and a fifteen-acre wood to explore. They allow 'camp anywhere' pitches and campfires so this one is perfect if you want to have a Ray Mears moment.

4. **Tresseck Campsite**, Hereford
    This is a great basic family campsite that allows those all-important campfires. Set on an old river meadow, there's

plenty of space for ball games and general larking about. Furthermore, what better way to spend a day than lazily paddling down the truly beautiful River Wye. You can hire canoes and launch right from the campsite.

5. **Tyllwyd Camping**, Ceredigion

    This small campsite lies along the banks of the River Ystwyth and is situated on the mountain road between Rhayader and Cwmystwyth, though you'll be lucky to see a car! Set amidst stunning mountain scenery you can relax in the peace and quiet of this valley of outstanding natural beauty. This is one of Kat's favourites because it's in the tiny picturesque village she grew up in. We recommend you take a walk through the Hafod estate, have a dip in the crystal clear waters of the River Ystwyth and take a walk up to Robbers' Cave for a spectacular view of a waterfall.

For further details, visit www.thehappycampers.co.uk.

Holiday Four: Canvas Chic
A week in a luxury yurt

Now this is the sort of camping that can't help but appeal. The word luxury helps. Even the name of the company that specialises in these holidays in the Ardeche in southern France – Canvaschic – makes the idea of camping more seductive to me. There are nine yurts with three communal cooking tents (one for each group of three yurts) with fully equipped kitchens, including cookers, pots and pans and crockery – so no need for a tin kettle and a gas burner. There are even fridges! And best of all, you don't need to take a sleeping bag – the yurts come complete with 'quality' bed linen, including duvets.

The idea behind Canvaschic was to offer holidays in the great and beautiful outdoors, sleeping under canvas, but without sacrificing comfort, style or space. The yurts themselves are a vision in cream and appear to have been designed by Ralph Lauren rather than Millets. For more information, go to www.canvaschic.com.

◉★◉★

Holiday Five: Eco Treats

There are plenty of ways to enjoy a trip off the beaten track without trampling all over it. Virginia Rowe edits one of my favourite websites, Style Will Save Us, and while she loves to travel the world, she does so on tippy-toe, and in a little luxury. Ethical holidays don't have to mean hard work, bunk beds and hairy blankets (although air con and power showers are hard to justify). Virginia's list of eco chic bolt-holes are a mix of cool riads, sci-fi snow pods, retro caravanning, and pure unadulterated pampering. Some are more far-flung than others. How you get there is between you and your own conscience. Just remember to tread lightly.

1. **La Rosa**: quirky campsite in Yorkshire (www.larosa.co.uk).
2. **The Sanctuary at Ol Lentille**: luxury hotel in Kenya (www.ol-lentille.com).
3. **BelRepayre Airstream & Retro Trailerpark**: 1950s fun in France (www.AirstreamEurope.com).
4. **Hix Island House**: modernist paradise in Puerto Rico (www.HixIslandHouse.com).
5. **Riad El Fenn**: cool Marrakech hotel (www.riadelfenn.com).
6. **Shompole** – luxury eco lodges in southern Kenya, for a safari experience that is created in harmony with the local flora,

fauna and people (www.shompole.com).

7. **North Island**: heavenly eco retreat in the Seychelles (www.north-island.com).

8. **White Pod**: Luxury Bond-esque camping in Switzerland (www.whitepod.com).

9. **Hotel Vigilius**: Mountain relaxation in Italy (www.vigilius.it).

10. **One to watch**: the world's first zero-carbon five-star resort is currently under construction in Zanzibar. It's designed by architects Richard Haywel Evans for Aquum, the brand behind some of the world's most luxurious resorts (www.peraquum.com).

Holiday Six: Surfing in Wales

If you really want to be at one with nature and let your hair down (or get it good and salty and tangled at least), you've got to try surfing. Howies have led the way in setting up an ethical surfing brand that we all want to wear. Here's their guide to the ten best surf spots in Wales:

1. Freshwater West (Pembrokeshire coast)
2. Llangennith (Gower Peninsula)
3. Hell's Mouth (Porth Neigwl)
4. Whitesands Bay (Pembrokeshire coast)
5. Rest Bay (Porthcawl)
6. Seven Bore (River Severn)
7. Caswell Bay (Gower Peninsula)
8. Newgale Sands (Pembrokeshire)
9. Barmouth (Snowdonia National Park)
10. Swansea (Glamorgan)

Holiday Seven: a Weekend in Brighton

It seems as though all roads (the ones with electric cars on them at least) lead to Brighton. An oasis for all things – and all people – ethical, it's the perfect place for a weekend away. Here are some tips from the designers and creative types who make it tick.

Kat Heyes: Andrew Fionda (of Pierce Fionda) has just opened a fantastic new vintage shop in Kemptown full of his finds and inspiration over the years. And the shop with no name next to the Kemptown Flea Market on St Georges Road has some fantastic vintage finds. It's run by a lady called Margaret, who is lovely . . . For second-hand bargains, check out Brighton Market at the railway station every Sunday from 6 a.m. Snoopers Paradise on Kensington Gardens; and Kemptown Flea Market on St Georges Road – brilliant for mooching round and picking up vintage finds for you and your home. For eating out, I recommend Terre a Terre, Brighton's leading vegetarian restaurant, with a delicious and inventive menu using local and often organic produce, and Due South, a small seafront restaurant with open kitchen, serving consistently great organic food and fresh-caught fish.

Enamore: My favourite organic eateries in Brighton are the Sanctuary in Hove and Bill's in the North Laines. Bill's does the most amazing desserts and breakfasts and is the best place to meet for business or pleasure. My favourite boutique has to be Narciste, off Sydney Street in the North Laines; they stock some great ethical labels like Matt & Nat bags and Junky Styling. I also love Snoopers Paradise for vintage clothing, accessories and home wares. I can get lost in there for hours!

Sarah Ratty, Ciel designer: I live in Brighton and see the horizon every day, which is so important. My favourite vintage shop is

Harlequin on Sydney Street (www.harlequin-vintage.co.uk). I must also recommend Bonafoodie for their wonderful range of local produce and organic food. Get your shoes from the ethical shoes boutique Last Shoes (www.lastfootwear.com). And pop into Jello on Gardner Street – it's the boutique where Cate Blanchett bought our Ciel coat, and is full of good stuff.

Hotel tip: Stay at Paskins Town House (www.paskins.co.uk) – a short walk away from the beach. This boutique B&B has a genuinely green approach, an Art Deco breakfast room, the odd four-poster bed, and award-winning organic (and vegetarian) food.

Holiday Eight: Flea around the World
A global guide to the ten best flea markets and thrift shops

Whether it's in Camden or Izmailovsky Park, a really great flea market is well worth travelling to (by boat, train, coach or bike, of course). Trekking round the world, gathering up its flea market junk, has to be one of life's great pleasures.

New York
The Annex Antiques Fair and Flea Market, Sixth Avenue between 25th and 26th Streets is a must-visit, and a way of life for the hippest New Yorkers. I've found some amazing clothes and accessories here, including bundles of 1950s fabric, a ball of pink sequins, and some fabulous 1930s silk pyjamas.

San Francisco
If you're in San Francisco on a Sunday, check out Alemany Flea Market, under the arches of Highway 280. A great place to pick up a bargain, you may find yourself

rummaging through a lot of junk, but there's some cool bohemian treasure too.

Paris
The flea market of St-Ouen sprawls between Porte de St-Ouen and Porte de Clignancourt and is open on Saturdays, Sundays and Mondays. It sells everything from antique clothes to tin bathtubs. It's huge and one of those places you are always guaranteed to spot a fashion designer or two haggling over a bit of lace or bias-cut dress. Make sure you continue under the underpass, because that's where all the really interesting stuff begins, with warehouses full of vintage beads, buttons and dress trimmings.

London
Like all good markets, Camden seems to keep on growing. Avoid the hippy tat and make for the stables and the cavernous shops under the railway arches. It's still possible to find a bargain.

Berlin
Die Nolle is housed in sixteen old railway trains at Nollen-dorfplatz, and boasts an eclectic mix of kitsch and recent history.

Amsterdam
Albert Cuyp Market in Amsterdam is great for new and second-hand clothes, clogs and waffles.

Lisbon
The Feira da Ladra, Campo de Santa Clara, Alfama, translates as Market of Female Thieves. This is a really brilliant market, where you can find anything from

beautiful vintage lace clothes, bags and sunglasses, to fabulous sequined dresses. Still unbelievably cheap. Open on Tuesdays and Saturdays.

Sydney
The Rocks Flea Market is more of an artisan market than a place to buy lovely old junk. Look for one-of-a-kind aboriginal pieces and textiles.

Tokyo
Ameya Yokocho is a serious market packed with old clothes, jeans and interesting finds, alongside fruit, veg and lots of brightly coloured plastic stuff.

Moscow
The Izmailovsky Souvenir Market is an experience – more theatre than market. You'll find Russian dolls, jewellery, and even a pair of Scandinavian mittens. Super cheap, but the dancing bears and bear steaks will offend animal lovers.

If you're keen to get off the well-trodden tourist map, or curious to see more of your own country, style consultant extraordinaire and co-editor of *Cheap Date*, **Kira Jolliffe**, insists that thrifting makes great tourism. Plus, you'll pick up some bargains in the process. She recommends you:

* Seek out little villages that you wouldn't normally visit and make a beeline for the church fete.
* Treat thrifting as a pastime.
* Daydream while you sift – it makes the whole process more creative.
* Remember your genetic foraging urges – the appreciation of colour and texture, the thrill of the find, and the competitiveness!

Kira's top charity buys

- Classic camel coat (actually cashmere) from Traid: £2.
- Alexander McQueen, perfect fit, dark brown, unworn dress, All Aboard, London W2: £5.
- Black velvet Windsmoor jacket with gold piping, Sue Ryder sale, Nettlebed, Oxon: £1.
- 1920s leather music case, St Mary Abbott's Church summer fete, W8: £4.
- Charcoal grey men's cashmere V-neck, Oxfam, Henley-on-Thames, Oxon: £15.
- Plain red cowboy boots, New Mexico thrift store: $4.
- Black leather Agnès b mini-skirt with thick zip up the side, Red Cross, SW6: £20.

Holiday Nine: New York, New York

At first glance, Manhattan might not seem to be the most eco friendly of places but, like most big cities pumping out enough pollution to poison a small planet, it has a thriving eco scene. To get to the core of it, I asked **Anne Burstein**, chic owner of the city's favourite ethical boutique Gominyc, to let us inside the Big Apple's conscience. Here's what she said:

A great vintage shop, which has two locations, one in the East Village near my store and one in Williamsburg Brooklyn, is Amarcord. They have really done a great job of selecting and merchandising their vintage threads. If you're looking for great vintage at a fraction of the original price, dig deep at Beacons Closet. They have locations around town (www.beacons closet.com). Another really cool thrift store is Housing Works. They have awesome, high-end duds at a fraction of the original price – often new with the tags still on. They also have a great bookstore/café in SoHo. And furniture . . . All of the stuff is donated and the proceeds go to fight HIV and AIDS and homelessness. See www.housingworks.org.

In terms of big chains, the most obvious addition is the Whole Foods store on Houston Street, which is around 10 blocks away from my shop (www.wholefoodsmarket.com). Some call it an oasis. You can certainly find some crunchy organic clothes there, along with the usual supermarket offerings. I have the same mixed feelings about it that I have for all big chains, but now we're on the subject, it's worth mentioning two other giants that have really beefed up their organic selection: ABC Carpet and Home (www.abchome.com) has an awesome, eclectic and well-curated selection of organic and sustainable products and it's easy to spend hours wandering around the aisles (not that I can really afford anything in there). Another NYC staple for the latest edgy upmarket trends is Barneys. They are now collaborating with Loomstate for some private label eco duds and have a pretty decent selection of ethical clothing and goodies. I have a lot of label crossover with them. See www.barneys.com.

Holiday Ten: Spa Out

The easiest way to find your inner Zen is to treat yourself to a spa holiday with a yoga programme thrown in. Donna Karan, Fashion's First Lady of yoga, recommends some downtime in Parrot Cay, where she goes to relax, meditate and be at one with nature (I'm there already). If the idea of flying to the Caribbean upsets your karma, however, a pioneering yoga practice, Vajrasati Yoga (www.vajrasatiyoga.co.uk), is planning eco yoga holidays that can be reached by train – in Europe and North Africa (rather than the usual retreats in India). They will be doing this in collaboration with environmentally friendly yoga travel specialists, Free Spirit Travel.

Avoid Guilt Trips – Lose the Carbs

Ethical travel is all about enjoying the world responsibly. Think before you fly. Use alternative forms of transport wherever possible. The more and the further you fly, the more you contribute to global warming. For most of us, it's impossible to avoid air travel at some stage. In this case, consider flying long haul less often but staying longer when you're there. In other words, take fewer, longer holidays. And offset your CO_2 emissions. Ed Gillespie recommends saving 'the occasional long haul flight, every other year or so, for what George Monbiot refers to as "love miles" (visiting family or friends abroad)'.

Carbon offsetting is by no means a cure for climate change – sadly, there's no chance of buying our way out of the problem. In fact, many environmental campaigners, such as Friends of the Earth, find the whole practice suspect, insisting that it discourages individuals and corporations from cutting down on their travel in the first place. Once the carbon has been emitted into the atmosphere, you can't buy it back again. Ed Gillespie sees it as 'a bridging tool only that buys us a bit more time. There is a lot of dodgy calculation going on. Essentially it's like a "carry on business as usual with a get out of climate change jail free card"!'

But offsetting can generate funds for sustainable energy projects, which can only be a good thing. If you do decide to offset, check that the provider you choose uses internationally certified carbon credits. Climate Care has a very clear and easy to use website. It estimates that your round trip from London to New York will create 1.54 tonnes of CO_2 emissions and the cost to offset it will be £11.55. Eighty per cent of the funds now go towards sustainable energy projects designed to reduce carbon emissions – like treadle pumps for irrigation and generating wind energy – with 20 per cent going towards rainforest restoration (see www.climatecare.org).

Because of the need for rigour and transparency in the carbon market, there is a new global standard for offsetting, established by the Gold Standard. Find out more at www.cdmgoldstandard.org – and go to the links section of the Gold Standard site for an up-to-date list of premium vendors.

Wish you were here?

If you have the time on your idyllic retreat, don't forget to send a postcard to your MP. Let them know that you've taken responsibility for your greenhouse gas emissions, and encourage them to enact legislation making it easy for everyone to do the same.

8

Get a Life,
Get a Hobby

Get a Life, Get a Hobby

'The cure for boredom is curiosity. There is no cure for curiosity'

Dorothy Parker

Modern life can be so tiring, it's hardly surprising that after work most of us choose to collapse in front of the TV, surf the Internet (for an average of four hours a night) or relax with a takeaway and a rented movie. There doesn't seem to be a time when we're not busy; many of us have become permanently attached to our work by the umbilical cord that is the Blackberry. When we do have a free hour or two, we are desperate to make the most of it.

All this is great for the leisure industry, which is working hard to show us a good time in return for our hard-earned cash. But how much pleasure do we really get from drinking in some identikit chainstore pub, or eating out at Pizza Inc on a high street – any high street – near you. Ethical living is all about getting back to something a little more interesting and personal, away from the mainstream. If you haven't done so already, why not get yourself a hobby? It's great to discover what really makes you tick.

Get good at something that's nothing to do with your work and you might even find your true vocation in life. For Jenny Ambrose of the hemp underwear company, Enamore, sewing used to be a hobby, but now it's become her life. Now, when she wants to relax, she goes for a hike instead. It's a similar story for many of the other designers who've contributed to this book, and who make a living in green fashion.

According to Rachael Matthews, who fell in love with knitting, and went on to found the radical knitting club, Cast Off, in 2000, knitting used to be a domestic chore, more a necessity than a hobby. But since 'these days, it is no longer the most economically viable way to dress (as it costs more to buy the yarn to knit a jumper than it does to buy one off the peg)', people have begun to see its hidden attractions. 'Handmade items have more value, as love has been put into them. Also knitting can act as therapy in the fast world that we live in. The fact that it takes time means we have to slow down and relax. It breeds confidence. To know that you have made something from scratch yourself is a wonderful feeling. Not only do you care about the garment more but it's guaranteed better quality. Plus, you are not going to lose a hand-knitted sock in the washing machine.'

Unplug the TV, give yourself a chance to recharge and, hopefully, slow down your carbon emissions in the process. You will discover that being fashionably green is a walk in the park. And if walking isn't your thing, there are so many other ways to enjoy the good life: sew something, watch your garden grow, bake a loaf of bread, make some pancakes, get into capoeira, start a silk-worm farm, go for a bike ride, talk about books, or simply do nothing – the pleasures of navel gazing should not be underestimated!

First though, take a moment to unwind, and rest your eyes . . .

How to Slow Down

Take a nap

We all know how important it is to get our beauty sleep. But resting shouldn't be confined to nights. Done properly, there are few things more refreshing than a quick afternoon snooze.

It seems that anything shorter than twenty minutes is a power nap. Anything longer is a siesta. Both, according to scientists, are beneficial and restorative. The best time to nap is just after lunch. Take as much time as you can. If you can only spare five minutes, then just close your eyes (obviously somewhere quiet and not in the middle of a meeting). Even closing your eyes for twenty seconds gives you a rest. Twenty minutes will increase alertness, stamina and performance. An hour can leave you feeling groggy because you fall into proper, deep sleep, so best set an alarm, put your feet up, and enjoy your forty winks.

Make your own hammock

If you can't find the perfect place to nap, why not try making your own hammock? It's easy to do and even easier to swing in for the rest of the day, congratulating yourself on your handiwork. If you have a spare two hours, and two trees handy, then follow these instructions.

You'll need:

3 metres of fabric, at least 1 metre wide (old curtains will do)
Sewing thread
15 metres of very strong, non-stretchable rope
A sewing machine (or you can try sewing it by hand)
Scissors
Tape measure

Instructions:

* Cut the fabric to the width and length you need. One metre wide is good for the average-sized person, but you might want it to be wider if you fancy hiding inside your hammock or sharing it with a friend.
* Fold over the edges of the fabric twice and sew seams.
* Fold over the ends of the hammock between 5 and 7.5 cm and sew them, allowing enough space to pass the rope through each end. Sew through several times to ensure that your hammock is strong.

* Cut the rope in half and thread each half through the ends of the hammock to form a loop. Tie the hammock underneath some shady trees and relax.
* Test carefully before jumping in – I'm afraid safety isn't guaranteed!

Turn off the box

The anti-television campaign group White Dot (www.white dot.org) organises a mass TV turn-off week in Britain once a year (usually in April). They want to remind us that:

* Television won't give you experiences – it will rob you of them.
* By turning off, you get a chance to rediscover your own life – it's important to remember that you are interesting, and the things you and your friends do are more important than the things you watch others do on television.

It's a fine thing to plan your own TV turn-off week. Involve your neighbours and you may end up making a new friend. Put the world to rights. Or perhaps put up those shelves you've been meaning to fix for months.

Read a book

Once you've switched off the television – nasty, energy-guzzling appliance! – you'll be able to catch up with your reading. If you're a voracious reader, join a library or check out www.book crossing.com, which encourages book-lovers to share their favourite reads by leaving them on trains or buses for others to enjoy.

You could form a book club and make a social event of it. If you don't watch TV all year, you will save over £42 in electricity, which will buy you a whopping 21 Penguin Classics. You might be clueless when it comes to discussing *Big Brother*, but you will be an expert on Jane Austen.

If you are lucky enough to have a good local, independent bookshop, use it. They'll get to know you and your reading habits and it's always fun to check out the books – and local authors – that they recommend.

Another dying breed that needs to be supported is the second-hand bookshop – the sort of place where you can spend hours perusing dusty dust jackets and finding out-of-print gems. You might have to go to country towns and sleepy villages to find them as the rents in most cities have pushed them out. One of my favourites is Broadhursts in Southport. It's a rickety old shop – been there since 1926 – with a warren of rooms and a fireplace. The best thing about it – apart from the variety of books, some new, lots old – is that they wrap up your purchases neatly in brown paper and string.

Have a cup of tea

There is a lot of nonsense talked about tea and how to make the perfect cup. The main things to make sure about are that the water is freshly boiled and, of course, that you've only boiled the amount you need. Next time you are in the market for a kettle, check out the Eco Kettle, which measures out the water for you. If you have a tea bag (or a teaspoon of loose tea) per cup, you can't really go wrong. Let the tea brew to your required hue, and add milk last if you are brewing in a mug. Whether it's green, red bush, jasmine, white tea, or chamomile, just make sure it's Fairtrade. And that goes for your favourite biscuits too.

Bake a cake

Recipe for Fairtrade banana and chocolate muffins

This is a really easy and quick way to use up all those overripe Fairtrade bananas. You'll need just five minutes to prepare. Makes twelve.

Ingredients:

Two large Fairtrade bananas, mashed

A good handful of your favourite Fairtrade chocolate broken into
*   chunks (I quite like Green & Black's Maya Gold)*

75 g Fairtrade organic soft brown sugar

4 tbsp sunflower or olive oil

1 free range organic egg

125 ml buttermilk (or ordinary milk)

200 g organic self-raising flour

Method:

1. Preheat oven to Gas 5, 190 C, 375 F.
2. Mix together the bananas, choc chips, sugar and oil.
3. Beat in egg and milk.
4. Fold in flour.
5. Spoon into greased muffin tins and bake for 15–20 minutes.

Invite your neighbours round and eat while still warm.

How to Get into Shape
Go on a carbon diet

Forget size zero. Forget Atkins. The new diet in town is 'the Low Carbon Plan' – for girls (and boys) who want to reduce the size of their footprint.

If you concentrate on reducing your energy use, you'll be surprised at how easy it is to lose the first few carbs. You've already turned off the TV so that's a good start.

1. First, calculate your carbon footprint. This has become quite an industry in itself – all the carbon offset businesses offer a way of doing so – and there are endless books and websites that will help calculate the damage you are doing to the environment. Arm yourself with your electricity and gas bills, a calculator, and try the tips from Earthday Network (www.myfootprint.org).
2. Change just one of your lightbulbs to low energy and save yourself £9 per year in electricity (and 38 kilograms of CO_2) or £100 over the bulb's lifetime.
3. Turn off your lights when you are not using them, something our parents used to tell us all the time!
4. Turn down the thermostat by one degree (knit yourself a warm jumper, see page 194).
5. Do a spot of draught proofing (much more fun than watching TV). By installing draught proofing you could save up to £20 a year on your heating bills. You can save about 140 kg of CO_2 if you draught proof your home effectively.
6. Try washing your clothes on a cold wash – or if you think that's a little extreme, at 30 degrees.
7. Cut out the tumble-drying. Line-dry instead (on dry days, of course).
8. Buy a smaller car – and only use it when you really need to.

Our cars produce 11 per cent of the country's carbon emissions.

9. Invest in an Electrisave electricity meter (www.electri save.co.uk) that shows you at a glance how much you're using. Put your kettle on and watch the carbs fly.

10. Don't leave your gadgets, televisions, computers and freeview boxes on standby. Make sure you turn off your phone recharger as soon as it's finished.

Gym won't fix it

If you do want to lose weight, there are plenty of great ways to get into shape. Paying a hefty subscription to join your gym isn't one of them. It's too expensive – both for you and for the planet (modern gyms aren't exactly energy efficient). And, to my mind, there's something perverse about the whole practice: most of us think nothing of driving to the gym to get on a treadmill or exercise bike, or standing on the escalator on the way to our aerobics class.

Experts agree that the biggest calorific impact you can make is to change the way you get about: don't drive if you can cycle; don't cycle if you can walk; don't walk if you can run; don't use the lift if there's a staircase. Enjoy the great outdoors and opt for a more natural workout.

* Go for a walk. Check out www.walkit.com, a brilliant website that tells you how to get from A to B and how many carbon emissions you've saved in the process.
* Play a game of frisbee.
* Take a run.
* Do t'ai chi – a martial art best enjoyed early in the morning in your favourite park.
* Get into capoeira – this Brazilian art form incorporates elements of African culture including dance, music, acrobatics and various fighting forms. A spectacle to watch, it is becoming

increasingly popular to learn, thanks in part to the likes of model students, like Gisele Bundchen.

* Practise yoga. Get your eco-friendly yoga kit from Christy Turlington's Nuala collection for Puma. It includes pieces made from bamboo – a cool, stretchy material, perfect for exercising in. Gossypium has a seriously great collection, made from Fairtrade and organic cotton. And to complete the look, Eco Yoga's jute yoga mat is all you need.
* Ride a bike.

On your bike

Not only is cycling a quick, cheap and easy way to get about, it's achingly fashionable too. Celebrity two-wheelers include Daryl Hannah, Naomi Watts, Vivienne Westwood, Giles Deacon, Chloë Sevigny, George Clooney, and the governor himself, Arnold Schwarzenegger.

How to cycle in style
* If you want to wear something sporty, Patagonia is the best place for cycle shorts and tops. Howies has a 'Love Me Love My Bike' T-shirt and a line in belts made from recycled bike tyres . . .
* If you don't have a basket, panniers are really practical for carrying shopping and work stuff. Ortlieb are the kings of the waterproof pannier world (although they use polyester, so aren't the most environmentally friendly option).
* Freitag has the ultimate recycled messenger bag. Their courier bags – in all shapes and sizes – are made from tarpaulin, seat belts, inner tubes and used airbags. Not that you want to look like you are wearing your bike or anything, but Worn Again also makes bags from inner tubes, so don't throw your tubes or tyres away – they can be put to good use (www.wornagain.co.uk).
* For the quintessential English ladies' bike, The Princess Sovereign from Pashley (www.pashley.co.uk) is one of the best

traditional cycles in the world. Built by hand in Stratford-upon-Avon, and combining classic styling with irresistible features – including a 'ding dong bell', gold-rimmed mudguards and a saddle designed for someone with more flesh on her bottom than a greyhound – it features in the film *101 Dalmatians*, and is beloved by the likes of Manchester supermodel Agyness Deyn.

I love my bike
By Laura Bailey, model

66 I have always ridden my bike whenever I can, both when I lived in New York, and now back in London. I've even biked to black tie events and hidden my bike around the corner. Now I have a son he comes on the back. I don't have a fancy bike – just an old-fashioned black ladies' one. And I don't have a fancy kit either, though I am as safe as I can be with lights and helmet (although I do ride in heels, I usually keep to wedges!). I don't drag Luc on bike rides in the rain, but when I'm alone I don't care – there's always hair and makeup when I get to the shoot! 99

Electric Wheels
My other car's a G-Wiz
By Mark Eley, designer

66 I've always been into cars. It started when I was young and used to do the Gumball rally with my father.
I bumped into the PR for the G-Wiz and we got to chatting

about how Eley Kishimoto as a company were aware of green issues and came up with this idea of us designing a pattern for one of their cars.

There wasn't any money to be made, just some great promotion for everyone involved; they got to brighten up the car which, to be honest, was the original ugly betty, and we got to let everyone know that we were into going greener, plus they gave us one of the cars to drive around in for a while.

We did three versions of the flash motif and each was a limited edition of thirty. We got together with some other eco car manufacturers like the biofuel Saab, and took them on the Gumball rally. We wanted to do it with as few emissions as possible.

I've got kids and they love it. In fact, most kids from the ages of two to thirteen point and get excited about the car because of its unique shape and flash down the side. It's great to drive, like riding a bumper car. We can fit in two adults and three kids; it's a bit crushed but the kids don't mind. It's a really fun car to be in.

Do Something Different . . .
Take action

One of my favourite websites – www.wearewhatwedo.org – inspires 'people to use their everyday actions to change the world'. Their list of simple, everyday actions makes the business of saving the earth seem remarkably easy, and actually rather fun. Change number one is to decline plastic bags. Their latest book, *Change the World 9–5*, gives fifty actions you can take during your working day. What makes it so appealing is that these really are things we can all do very easily, without too much sacrifice, and without so much as lifting a placard.

Make a pledge

If you have your own ideas for action – whether it's going on a protest, raising money, starting a petition, or making a lifestyle change – you can get support and galvanise community action through the Pledge Bank: www.pledgebank.com. This is a great site, and so easy to use. All you need to do is log your pledge and the number of people you want to see alongside you, and see what happens. Site successes (pledges that have achieved the required numbers of supporters) include giving up chocolate, writing a letter to Primark, and using sustainable transport.

Volunteer

Now that you're in the community spirit, why not try volunteering – it's a surprisingly fun option, and proven to help reduce stress and depression. Of course, working at Oxfam might not be the most glamorous thing you can imagine signing up for, but just think of the opportunities you'll have to grab the best bargains before they go out on the shop floor.

If you want to combine volunteering with more specialist fashion work experience, Traid are always looking for help, either in the shops or on the sorting floor. If you love clothes, you might enjoy it. And if you can sew, you might find yourself helping out with the Traid Remade refashioning programme (see page 98).

Guerrilla gardening

Digging at midnight, 'fighting the filth with forks and flowers', the guerrilla gardening movement is gathering momentum around the world, from Swansea to San Diego. If you're upset by the neglect of our public spaces, want to improve the aesthetic of your city, make the countryside that

little bit more colourful, or simply don't have a garden of your own and want to meet some green-fingered friends, find out how to get involved at www.guerrillagardening.org.

Grow Something
Start a jungle in your back garden

OK, maybe not a jungle, but bamboo grows fast, so fast – up to one and a half metres a day – it is effectively seen as a weed in some places in Japan. Approximately 40 million hectares of the earth is covered with bamboo, mostly in Asia. About 200 million tonnes are harvested annually. The strongest-growing woody plant on earth – potentially stronger than steel – it is also one of the most sustainable materials we have. The variety of uses, the ease with which it grows and the fact that its clumping nature enables a lot of it to be grown in a comparatively small area, makes it one of the cheapest, most sustainable and efficient crops.

More and more, designers are seeking it out, and not just for children (who will love Tatty Bumpkin's bamboo T-shirts), and yoga clothes, but for furniture, floors – even underpants (look for the latter at Jenny White's Eco Boudoir).

There's no special technique involved in growing bamboo: just plant, water generously for the first year, and then leave to grow . . . and grow.

The furniture designer Tom Dixon is on a mission to bring bamboo into our homes. As creative director at Artek, he has introduced a bamboo table and chairs (used in a similar way to birch plywood), which look set to become instant classics. He says, 'you have to use bamboo in good confident sheets to stop it looking rustic. And it can sometimes be a bit yellow, so it's best if it is pale. We live in hope that more people will use it.'

Start your own silkworm farm

This isn't one of the easiest undertakings, or one of the most enticing (bugs are really unattractive), but sometimes it's nice to try a new hobby – and set yourself a bit of a challenge too.

At the time, growing a silkworm farm at my home in east London made perfect sense. We'd been looking for a suitable pet for an asthmatic, I was researching the production of silk, goldfish seemed a bit obvious . . . and the silk caterpillars sounded cute. Apparently they would be very responsive. According to one authority: 'They look up when you enter the room because they anticipate you feeding them . . . After the final moult, they enjoy crawling on your hands and exploring . . .'

I sobered up slightly when it came to ordering the kit (from www.just-green.com). The picture on the website shows a little dish with some ugly white grubs in it. I started to doubt how much love and affection these worms would give me, in return for my feeding them their synthetic mulberry leaves each day. They have voracious appetites so I looked for a mulberry tree to plant in the garden, but they only feed on white mulberry leaves, which are impossible to find.

I still doubt that I will get on to the spinning and weaving stages with my silkworms. I asked my friends at Cast Off for advice, and it seems that I will need two to three thousand cocoons to produce a pound of silk. If I want to make a kimono, I'll need 2100 silkworm moths. Not sure what the neighbours would make of that – although apparently the adult moths can't fly.

And why persist with this grow-your-own silk experiment? Because it transpires that commercial silk production is innately cruel. Silk might be biodegradable, renewable, organic, and even fair trade. But the traditional production process still requires that moths never leave the cocoon alive. In order to prevent damage to the thread, the larvae are boiled or roasted alive – silkworm cocoons are baked at about 100 degrees centigrade for over two hours, which kills the worms and also makes the cocoons easy to unravel without breaking the thread. And there we were, thinking silk was a lovely natural ethical fibre.

Happily, for vegans, and those worried about being reincarnated as a silkworm in the next life, there is an alternative. Peace silk, also known as vegetarian silk, is raised and processed differently. The moths are allowed to emerge from their cocoons to live out their full life cycle. The silk is degummed and spun like any other fibre, instead of being reeled. The resulting yarn is soft, fluffy, and light like a cloud. You can buy selected items from Peta, the Natural Store and Denise Bird (see the Little Green Book for website details).

Of course, the killing of the moth chrysalis doesn't bother everyone, which might be why I'm alone in this hobby. But the idea of a silkworm farm in east London isn't so ridiculous. In the 1680s Spitalfields became the centre of the silk industry in England. In the 1820s 20,000 home looms for silk weaving provided work for 50,000 Londoners. The traditional Spitalfields silk weavers could not compete with machine production and, by 1910, 95 per cent of the skilled workers had been forced out of employment. The last record of silk weaving in east London was of four silk weavers in Fournier Street in 1930.

Grow your mind,
By Pearl Lowe

❝ I love to meditate and do yoga. In fact I meditated through the birth of my youngest daughter, eighteen months ago. Having a baby while 'sober' was incredibly spiritual. I'm off all drugs and I didn't want any funny stuff. With all my previous births I was screaming 'Give me drugs! Anything you've got!'

Suzanne Howlett, my healer, also delivered my child; she taught me to meditate. All my other births had been so bad, but even without the drugs the last was the best. Suzanne is wonderful. She blends me special oils, which I'm obsessed with. Her oils are pretty amazing. When I was pregnant she gave me a birthing blend. One night when I was pregnant I had a bad back, so I got Danny up in the middle of the night and he rubbed this oil on me. I went into labour the next day, one month early. When I told Suzanne about this, she swore it was the oil that induced the birth.

For more info, see www.divinelynurtured.co.uk (please check with your doctor before using any oils in pregnancy).

●★●★

Get Creative

 How to start a knitting circle,
By Rachael Matthews, Cast Off

Nothing could be simpler than setting up your own knitting circle. All you need is one other friend who can knit, a big basket full of spare needles and yarn, and two friends who can't knit but want to learn. Then the four of you go to the pub and the two of you teach the two who can't knit, then slowly everyone in the pub will want to know what is going on. Spread the spare needles around and before you know it everyone is knitting and you've built up a gang, so you collect everyone's emails and start a mailing list and arrange to meet somewhere different next time.

My best tip for a successful knitting circle is to always go somewhere public. If you stay at people's houses it becomes clingy and competitive, whereas the whole point is to attract new people in. You will be surprised at how much interest you get. Knitting in public brings strangers together from all walks of life. Everyone has their own knitting story and they are always happy and nostalgic.

To find your nearest local knitting circle, go to www.stitch nbitch.co.uk or keep an eye on Cast Off's 'cosy chat' page: www.castoff.info. Good topics of conversation while you knit and natter include the latest creations of the knitterati, Julia Roberts, Madonna and Russell Crowe. Yes, they all love knitting too.

In the loop

* Be Sweet does knitting with a conscience. The yarn is handspun and dyed by the Xhosa women in the Eastern Cape, South Africa, a job creation programme that enables them to support their extended families in an economically depressed region with 75 per cent unemployment and little opportunity aside from hard labour in the pineapple fields. Proceeds from Be Sweet yarns and products go towards local projects including funding the local school. Also, the range of colours and yarns are truly scrumptious so you can't go wrong. See www.besweet products.com.

* North London's knitting shop, Loop, holds classes in everything from knitting socks, 'experimental knitting', Julie Arkell's fantastic make-your-own-creature workshops, and knitting and crochet classes for children. It also sells the most seductive array of gorgeous yarns and natural dyes, and eco yarns ranging from alpaca to organic cotton. Everything is available to buy online too. Even if you don't knit, you are guaranteed to fall under its spell. Check out www.loop.gb.com.

* Barley Massey is a textile designer with a particular interest in recycling and the environment. Her east London shop sells everything you need to be a conscientious knitter, as well as a range of products made from recycled materials. For more, see www.fabrications1.co.uk.
* One for the boys: www.menwhoknit.com.
* You can knit your own cakes – much better for you than eating them – by downloading patterns from www.trulyscrumptious knittedfood.co.uk.
* www.hipknits.co.uk is a great resource for knitters, with some interesting specialist wools and yarns, including recycled silk from shredded sari remnants in Nepal. The silks come in a range of jewel-like colours and are spun by women in Nepal, many of whom are refugees or have been abandoned, or rescued from forced prostitution.
* For first-hand advice, go to Cast Off's shop, Prick Your Finger, in London's Bethnal Green (www.castoff.info).

Make your own presents

I have a friend, Kate, who makes her own Christmas presents every year. They are always amazing, and I imagine she must start doing it around September. One year, there was a fantastic bolster cushion. Another it was a set of chic coasters, made from homemade felt. And I still use the really gorgeous shoe bags she made from beautiful printed silk (sorry, silkmoths). Nothing I buy can ever come close to the presents she gives. When I gave birth to my daughter, she even made an amazing cosy blanket, edged in satin ribbon, with Sybilla's initial immaculately chain-stitched on to it. This really is something money can't buy. It's about the time and care she has put into every perfect stitch. Some years, she does get a bit stressed around December time. But probably not as stressed as the rest of us rushing round, mindlessly Christmas shopping, buying stuff for the sake of it.

Ideas to make and give

* Simple lavender bags (if you can grow your own lavender, even better).
* Homemade biscuits. Look out for old tins at charity shops to put them in.
* Socks. Suddenly they are an original present if you can knit your own!
* Plant up interesting old containers with hyacinth bulbs (this is very easy).
* Pompom jewellery. Once you've mastered the art of making pompoms (see page 86) you won't be able to stop. String them up to make colourful necklaces for your friends.

How to make old fabrics into new cushions

Be inspired by the fashion designer Rifat Ozbek, who makes the most luxurious and exquisite cushions out of the fabrics he has collected over the years, and on his travels around the world. His shop, Yastikistanbul (yastik means cushion in Turkish), is in Bodrum in Turkey (www.yastikistanbul.com), and sells only cushions – of all shapes and sizes and in an ever-changing selection of patterns and prints. A cushion is, he says, a luxury, a reminder of a memory or a dream.

You can easily make your own, using up scraps of fabric you might have collected and don't want to throw away, or even fabric from old clothes, blankets or curtains that you can no longer use. It's a good way of keeping things that have sentimental value too – old clothes you can't wear any more but don't want to throw away.

Bags and
Shoes

9

Bags and Shoes

'I did not have three thousand pairs of shoes. I had one thousand and sixty' Imelda Marcos

'If I don't stop shopping, I'll end up a bag lady; a Fendi bag lady, but a bag lady . . .' Carrie Bradshaw, *Sex and the City*

You Can never Have enough Bags . . .

Fashion used to be about clothes. Now it's all about shoes. And bags. Bags and shoes . . . The more expensive, it seems, the better. Apparently, we just can't get enough. The thing is, you don't have to think too much with accessories. Right? You don't have to worry about looking fat with a bag (especially a super-sized one). You don't have to stress about changing rooms to sling on a pair of heels. You don't even have to think about what goes with what. The best shoes and bags go with everything, add instant glamour to any outfit, and even outlast the season. That's what makes them such a great investment.

Of course, ethically, there is so much more to it than that. It's easy to fall in love with beautiful things, but there are plenty of questions we should ask before committing to the big purchase. This chapter will help you accessorize with sustainable style. It will look at which bags are rubbish and which are for life. It will consider the question of leather – ethical or not? It will tell you what to shop for, what to put your shopping in, pave the way for lighter footprints, and, in case you're feeling creative, show how to make your own designer arm candy – now there's a statement worth making!

The It Bag – a dangerous addiction?

I don't know about you, but I've lost track of what designer bag I'm supposed to be wearing this week. Is it a Muse? A Paddington? A Spy? I know it's definitely not a Baguette – that was the bag, made by genius bag designer, Sylvia Fendi, that started the It Bag craze at the end of the 1990s. It's probably due a revival, of course.

The whole bag thing just makes my head spin. When Balenciaga's Lariat bag first came out, Nicole Ritchie bought it in green, blue, pink, black and white. Louis Vuitton's latest incarnation – the Marilyn – comes with its own wardrobe in the form of a trunk, complete with thirty-three compartments and a different lipstick-coloured bag to fit in each one. You may rest assured, however, that even Louis Vuitton believes there are only five such conspicuous bag consumers in the world, because that's all they've made.

Although the fashion houses are still enjoying the increase in revenue from the bag market – recent Mintel research has shown that we spend £350 million on handbags every year in the UK alone, an increase of nearly 150 per cent in just five years – the situation has kind of got out of control. These days, celebrities get snapped because of the bag they are carrying. And within minutes, those pictures are being zapped to the desktops of fashion editors around the world, to high street retailers keen to get the look, and on to the pages of the weekly fashion zines, where they will be analysed and pored over for hours by picture editors, fashion insiders and us, the consumers.

So Kate Moss is hauling the latest YSL Muse around with her. Is this really news? I would like to let you in on a secret. I can't imagine Kate has bought a handbag in her life. In the past year alone she has been seen with the Luella Stevie, Mulberry Emmy, Mulberry Roxanne, YSL Muse, Chloé Betty, Marc Jacobs Stam and a Burberry Manor (which sold out after three weeks). And they are only the ones she's been photographed with. The exposure is like gold dust for any fashion house. The cash tills go ker-ching!

That's why all those girls – from Mischa Barton to Gwyneth Paltrow – have an endless supply of new bags. Did you really think they bought them like everyone else? If they did, they wouldn't change them as often as their underwear. So take a deep breath, and think about the bags you have bought in the past twelve months – or even the bags that you have simply lusted after. Ask yourself, was it worth the money? Was it really worth trying to keep up? After all, you are at such an unfair disadvantage.

If you haven't bought the real thing, have you been tempted by the high street rip-offs? Or even a fake? (They can be incredibly realistic looking.)

Faking it

The fashion houses will tell you that fake designer goods are unethical. And tempting though it is to dismiss this, and shell out a tenner in the market for a 'Louis Vuitton', they're right.

Buy a fake and you become the end of a chain that is supporting all manner of criminal behaviour, from drug trafficking to terrorism. According to Interpol, counterfeiting and piracy – a global trade worth some $250 billion – is rapidly becoming the preferred method of funding for terrorist groups. By buying a counterfeit bag, you could be putting money into the coffers of terrorist groups, or funding other organised crime. And chances are, your fake will have been manufactured in the Far East, produced by women and children, held slavishly, in unmonitored, appalling conditions.

How to tell if it's a fake:
* If it's on sale on eBay for £50 'buy it now', alongside twenty others from the same seller. Basically, if you can't believe the price, then don't.
* If it's on sale at your local street market, bearing the letters LV.

You know it's a fake – why are you even asking?

* The exterior might look convincing, but check the lining. Most serious bag brands will have their insignia woven into the lining.
* Check the zippers. Prada has a little toggle at the end of their zippers; Hermès, who bought the first zip license in France in the 1920s, boasts a discreet H on all of its zips.
* Handles wrapped in tissue or bubble wrap. A sure sign of a fake.
* Louis Vuitton bags are made from one continuous piece of fabric so if you find one with a seam across the bottom, it's not the real thing.

How to hire a handbag

You don't have to keep on buying to keep up with the latest celebrity bag. A far more economical way is simply to hire the latest arm candy. Joining a bag library is a bit like using the car pool lane on the motorway. Borrow a Marc Jacobs Hobo for a month, then send it back so that someone else can use it. And you can indulge your desire to have a bag like Gwen Stefani's one month and Liz Hurley's the next without bankrupting yourself – and adding to the world's ever-increasing bag mountain while you are at it. Check out www.fashionhire.co.uk and www.bagaddiction.co.uk.

It Bags that Won't Date

If you are determined to buy one to-die-for bag in your lifetime, then there are models I would recommend you splurge on. A really well-made luxurious leather bag is a thing to behold, and it's not something you will be tempted to replace every few months.

I remember my mum's handbag that she used for most of the 1970s and 1980s (it survived not just maxis, minis, power suits and sportswear, but through two entire decades!). It was a patchwork affair – black and purple – with elegant leather straps that hooked over her shoulder. It smelt of face powder and Chanel No 5, and only finally gave up the ghost when one of the straps frayed and broke. She was relieved when it finally died and she could buy a new one, but she would never have dreamt of changing it for another if she hadn't had to. Not because she didn't want to, but because it was 'a good leather bag'. It wasn't Hermès or anything, but it was obviously well made enough to withstand years of abuse.

So I would say, if you can afford a classic Chanel 2.55 quilted bag, then go for it. You will be the envy of all your friends – of all ages – and you will never need to buy another handbag again. Likewise, if you are in the market for a Hermès Birkin, don't waste a minute. Get on that list! You will have an heirloom that will be handed down from mother to daughter (or son if the inclination takes him) for generations. It's a great investment too – almost as good as a pension plan.

Classic arm candy

Hermès Birkin
The No. 1 It Bag of all time, this is the holy grail of all handbags.
(see page 24 for more).

Chanel 2.55
If you like to think of yourself as a bag aficionado, then you really
need to know about this bag. The 2.55 from Chanel was first
introduced in February 1955 (hence the 2.55) by the ever-practical
Coco, who wanted a hands-free bag with a shoulder strap. To
celebrate its sixtieth birthday, Chanel reintroduced the 2.55 in
2006 with a special stamp inside.

Gucci Jackie O
Gucci has many classics but the one Jackie Onassis chose is
probably the one that will stand the longest test of time.

Chloé Paddington
One of the world's most (badly) copied bags. One of designer
Phoebe Philo's golden moments at Chloé. Every single one of the
8000 Paddingtons produced for spring 2005 were spoken for
before they reached the shops.

Mulberry Bayswater
Mulberry calls the Bayswater their 'all rounder'. This is their most
covetable classic and a big hit with celebrities like Kate Moss, who's
often seen out with her black version.

Fendi Spy
The Fendi S/S 06 Spy bag's notorious status is caused partly by its
enormous waiting list, which can last up to three years, so you have
to be sure you want to commit to it for longer than a season.

Louis Vuitton Never Full

Every time Louis Vuitton makes a bag it seems to be a new classic.
The latest wittily named Never Full, however, has all the hallmarks
of a bag for life. It is made in the classic monogram canvas, and is
named because it is so capacious it is never full.

If you simply cannot afford a designer It Bag, or the thought of
such indulgence turns your stomach, the ethical and inspired
choice would be to make your own. Ciel's award-winning designer
Sarah Ratty has provided us with a wonderful, easy-to-follow
pattern.

How to knit your own arm candy
By Sarah Ratty, designer

*   Choose your length of
    fabric. You will probably
    need approximately 5
    metres of cloth, which can
    be cut from anything –
    old dress fabrics,
    remnants, favourite jeans,
    old T-shirts – a colourful
    mixture or same-
    colour/different-cloth
    medley (I have used
    some old denim
    lengths we had in the
    studio).

1. Cut fabric lengths into 1"
strips. old curtains,
random fabric lengths from
the market etc old favourite
dresses... old T-shirts -

* Cut the cloth into one-inch strips, knot the lengths together and roll into a ball; you will need to make approximately 500 metres of yarn in this way, which is about five chunky balls.

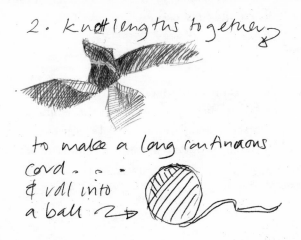

2. knot lengths together

to make a long continuous
cord . . .
& roll into
a ball

* Then, using 15 mm needles, cast on 21 stitches and knit for 25 rows or until work measures 55 cm (or twice required length of bag). Cast off.

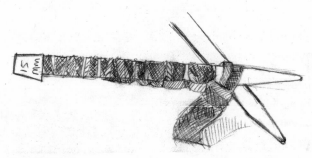

3. Using size 15 mm needles
cast on 21 stitches. . .

4. Knit 25 rows in
plain knit. until
work measures
55 cm (or twice
required length.)

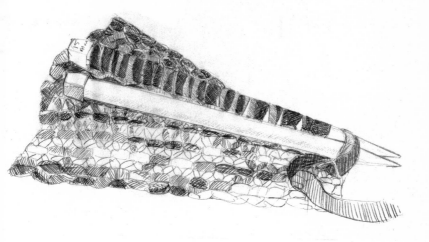

*   Fold work in half and sew folded edges together. Make the
    strap by plaiting three ends of three lengths together and
    attach to the bag.

*   You can be as creative as you like and embellish the bag with
    pompoms or rosettes made out of fabric scraps, buttons . . .

* You can make different lengths of bags or clutch bags, shoulder bags depending on the length of the fabric knitted. Ours measures 25 cm square when finished and is a small bag that fits high under the arm. You can stitch a couple of buttons with loops to close it, use press studs or sew in a short zip. The most important thing is to exercise your imagination and have fun!

* Be creative and enjoy.

If you're not confident with needles, but are keen to get your 'own label' bag, try getting your design or photo screenprinted on to an environmentally friendly bag at www.bagsby.co.uk.

Alternative It Bags

Made in Ethiopia

Once upon a time (around the turn of the twentieth century), there was an empress who ruled Ethiopia. Her name was Taytu. And if she was still alive today, she would be very proud of the luxurious handbags that are being made in her name. No doubt, she would have worn them wherever she went – rather like Margaret Thatcher and her trademark bag in the 1980s.

Luxury goods are not something we associate with one of the hungriest, poorest countries in the world. But that is exactly what a group of Ethiopian companies who specialise in leather are producing – with backing from the United Nations, no less.

The first Taytu collection was showcased fresh from Addis Ababa in Paris in 2006, focusing on leather bags, but also including shoes, jewellery and other accessories. With the help of an experienced accessories designer from Italy, twelve manufacturers have produced a collection that fuses Ethiopian handicrafts and techniques with a Western sensibility. And the results are impressive – the bags have a certain Marni aesthetic about them, in lovely, soft, muted colours and organic shapes and patterns. For more, see www.taytu.com.

Bags of irony

Put your tongue in your cheek and have a look at the brilliant counterculture fashion and accessories line **Slow and Steady Wins the Race**. Mary Ping set up her company in New York in 2001, and designs according to an anti-consumerist manifesto, creating compelling garments from the most inexpensive fabrics and materials. To minimise the waste of the fashion cycle, Ping limits her collection's production to 100 of each item, and concentrates on affordable, timeless pieces. Her calico bags are like production samples, paying homage to classic models. Choose from the 'Balenciaga', 'Birkin', 'Chanel' or 'Gucci'. Each one is reduced to the basic shape, outline and key attributes. The Dior Gaucho, for example, has a plain hardware store D-ring hanging off it.

●★◉★

Can You Wear Leather and Call Yourself a Vegetarian?

So you are a vegetarian who wears leather. Join the club. I haven't eaten meat for most of my adult life – ever since I saw that poussin in the fridge at Sainsbury's. It was so tiny and it seemed like such a waste of a life. Plus, I'd just seen David Lynch's weird dancing chickens in his oddball film *Eraserhead*. So it happened overnight that I stopped eating meat. But leather shoes and bags have been a more complex matter. I couldn't suddenly just chuck out all my shoes. To be perfectly honest, I've only recently started to think it is an issue.

Vegetarian alternatives

Although I do still buy the odd pair of leather shoes, I subconsciously opt for pairs made of anything but. Camper are a great non-leather option – the Mallorcan brand always has a good pair of something canvas and colourful. Ask for Camaleons. (In fact, my all-time favourite shoes are a pair of traditional Mallorcan peasant shoes, made from canvas off-cuts, string and tractor tyres. I've worn them every summer for over a decade. And I promise, they don't smell!). I also have a pair of plastic Birkenstock clogs which might not be everyone's cup of Café Direct, but I doubt they will ever wear out, and the insoles are replaceable if they do. They are great for when it rains or if you want to go for a walk in a muddy field. Not ideal for tea at the Ritz, mind.

I have to say that the combination of the words 'handmade' and 'ethical' often strike fear into my heart. Handmade, ethical shoes are often not worth looking at, unless you really don't care what your feet look like. I'm all for a pair of Birkis. Or even a pair of No Sweat's brilliant hemp hi-tops. But those shoes that are designed with only ethics and hobbits in mind really don't do the cause any favours. And there are plenty of them. I know they are doing their bit for the environment, but really – our feet deserve better. Here are some alternatives:

* **Stella McCartney**'s natural raffia, woven heels are divine.
* For the Brighton-based **Beyond Skin**, cruelty-free shoes are an art form. There's something for every occasion, whether you are meeting the Queen, getting married, or off for a night on the town.
* American, cruelty-free shoe pioneers **Charmone** are embraced by the mainstream – it's hard not to love their colourful, exotic-looking platforms and thongs.

* **Novacas** (it means 'no cows') is a Portuguese vegan shoe company with a charming website www.novacas.com, and some really tempting shoes.
* **Worn Again** are on a mission to make the definitive ethical trainer. Set up in 2003, the brand is a collaboration between inspirational activists Anti-Apathy and Terra Plana. Instead of all those nasty high-tech synthetics, the company uses recycled materials for the uppers – everything from fireman's jackets to car seats and old blankets – and recycled rubber for the soles.
* **Terra Plana** won the *Observer*'s Ethical Fashion Product of the Year Award 2007, making some of the most innovative, ethical and fabulous shoes on the market.

Beyond fabulous

For vegan Natalie Dean, leather shoes became such a no-no that she decided to make her own. Dismissing the alternatives on the market as far too worthy and unfashionable, she rang her friend, the shoe designer Olivia Morris and over a few beers in the pub, Olivia told her everything – well, as much as she could – about setting up a shoe business. Beyond Skin – a cruelty free, ethical shoe collection – was born. And today the shoes are worn by the likes of Natalie Portman – who knows a good thing when she sees it. In fact, when Ms Portman mentioned the brand in an interview in *Vanity Fair*, Beyond Skin received thirty orders from America in one week. Look out Manolo, the veggies are coming!

I can't believe they're not leather! What the stars wear

You'd be surprised how many celebrities opt for non-leather shoes when they're out and about – even on the red carpet.

* Gwyneth Paltrow would rather go barefoot than wear leather –

but then it helps when you're best mates with Stella McCartney.

* Natalie Portman loves her heels by Charmone and, of course, Beyond Skin.

* Thandie Newton loves her shoes full stop, and was snapped recently wearing Georgina Goodman's amazing recycled tin shoes (see below).

* Taupe Hynde recommends Vegetarian Doc Martens and Brothel Creepers from www.vegetarian-shoes.co.uk and Payless (in the US) for vegan.

* Joaquin Phoenix is a committed vegan. He even went as far as to make sure the cowboy boots he wore to play Johnny Cash were leather-free.

How to make a pair of sandals from a drinks can

Next time you recycle your Sprite cans (or should that be your cans of organic Guarana), try to imagine how they could be recycled into the most incredible pair of haute couture shoes. No really. Because that's just what the shoe designer, Georgina Goodman, has done. Like the fairy godmother in Cinderella, she waves her magic wand and out of two and a half drinks cans, she can make the most amazing pair of shiny, futuristic aluminium sandals, by simply cutting and stitching them together on to the softest leather.

'I love recycling and metal is one of the most environmentally friendly materials as every drinks can is one hundred per cent recyclable,' she says. 'It can also be recycled infinitely so technically I could produce an entirely new pair of shoes for next season by melting down this pair! Bare metal is also a very interesting material to work with as it has a wonderful texture and is incredibly versatile and flexible – perfectly adaptable to the shoe making process.'

The heels are made of cast aluminium, and Georgina has even made use of the pull tabs as tassels. These really are shoes fit for an eco princess. For environmentalist and shoe fetishist Thandie

Newton, the aluminium sandals were the perfect fit. She chose to wear hers where she wears all her favourite heels, on the red carpet. Look out next time you see her photographed – she may well be wearing them, as, conscious of waste, she makes sure she gets good wear out of her stuff.

The ethical It Bag

Of course, unless you've got an entourage to carry your stuff for you, you'll need a 'vegetarian' bag to go with those shoes. If you're off leather, there are still plenty of labels to lust after:

Matt & Nat, the cruelty-free bag brand from Montreal, is on a mission to make synthetic, faux-leather bags cool, and provide a dose of good karma in the process. Their bags even come with a 'positivity' message stamped on the lining: 'Choose life, choose positivity, choose the golden rule, choose to be at peace with yourself, choose salvation.'

Check out the range at **Funkifish**, set up by designer Marie-Bernadette Young. Young does all sorts of creative things with fish skins, including a range of Mermaid bags. The psychedelic, iridescent ones are really quite cool (they'll certainly get you noticed) and don't smell fishy at all.

Go for canvas or other fabrics. As Anya Hindmarch has proved with her 'I'm not a plastic bag' shopper, you don't need leather to create an It Bag. **Ollie & Nic** make some great bags using materials like corduroy, and hessian. Look out for the ones without leather trim.

If you want to splurge, **Stella McCartney**'s Ladybird is the only designer option that lets you be stylish, ethical and kind all at the same time. It's made from vinyl (that's the compromise you'll have to make) and is sold in Stella's wind-powered London store.

Stella also has a 'no leather or animal products' clause written into her contract with Gucci. She uses a mix of man-made, faux-leather and natural materials, all the while trying not to compromise on style. Look out for more veggie bags with her latest collaboration with Lesportsac.

Stella McCartney's take on leather

66 It's surprising to me that people cannot get their heads around a non-leather bag or shoe. They already exist out there, but unfortunately designers feel they have to slap a leather trim or sole on them. People need to start looking at the product, and if they like it, that's all that matters. If it has an ethical or ecological edge, that's a huge bonus. We address these questions in every other part of our lives except fashion. 99

The right sort of leather

Even if you're not vegetarian, it's still worth considering alternatives to leather. It's not the most ethical material, I'm afraid.

About 66 per cent of leather comes from cows. And according to the wise fount of all green knowledge, www.treehugger.com,

it takes 8 acres of land, 12,000 pounds of forage, 125 gallons of gasoline and other petroleum derivatives for fertiliser, 2500 pounds of corn, 350 pounds of soybeans, 1.2 million gallons of water and 1.5 acres of farmland (to grow the crops for feed), plus various insecticides, herbicides, antibiotics and hormones to grow one cow from an 80-pound calf to its full size, when it can be slaughtered and the hide harvested.

Basically, cow production is a pretty dirty and wasteful operation. And that's not to mention the problem of flatulent cows – each molecule of methane has twenty-one times as much global warming potential as a molecule of CO_2!

If you can't resist however, vege-tanned leather is far superior to the mineral (or chrome) tanned stuff. Natural and chemical free, the vegetable method employs tannin which occurs naturally in tree bark. Look out for:

* **Bill Amberg** – a total leather fanatic – uses incredibly high-quality vege-tanned leather.
* **Entermodal** produce a small range of designs in vegetable tanned leather that are elegant, timeless and made to be taken apart at the end of their life and upcycled into other products.
* **Mulberry** produce wonderful bags designed to stand the test of time and most of them are made with natural vege-tanned leather. The company is responsible for some of the most lusted-after bags in history (including the Roxanne and the Bayswater). 'Classic became a dirty word for a while in fashion, but now it's back,' said designer Stuart Vevers, after winning the British Designer of the Year Award in 2006. The company is introducing jute bags to replace its existing carrier bags – no doubt they will become as desirable as the bags they are designed to carry.
* RCA graduate **Inghua Ting** (www.tinglondon.com) makes bags, wallets and belts from recycled leather – mainly sourced from old belts and saddles. The results are surprisingly luxurious.
* For fantastic chrome-free leather shoes, look no further than **Terra Plana** – the company overseen by Galahad Clark of the Clarks shoe family. Their bestseller is a flat pump called

Mumbai, which is made from vege-tanned leather, with a Latex sole. Terra Plana has a system of symbols designed to guide you through all the processes it takes to make a pair of shoes. Their designs are light, sustainable and repairable, and use as much recycled and eco-friendly material as possible.

* What I like best is when a designer you love turns out to be ethical – even though they don't make it a selling point. **Shoefolk** is a big favourite of mine. The dyeing process is vege-based, resulting in lovely soft colours like moss green and warm grey. Their gorgeous quilted boots and shoes use quilts made by the Sami Tribe in Pakistan. And the shop on Lambs Conduit Street in London is fitted out with reclaimed wood. So lots of Brownie points all round.

* **Doc Martens** are launching a new green shoe, designed by Sarah Ratty of Ciel. With the footprint of an angel (the sole of the shoe leaves the imprint of angels' wings), this is easy-to-wear, functional footwear, with edge. The vege-tan leather boots have knitted organic Peruvian alpaca uppers (a bit like built-in legwarmers). The soles are made from sustainable rubber, and stitched with a filling of rice husks. They are so biodegradable, I worry they might dissolve in a heavy rainstorm!

The Evils of Plastic

So now you've got your ethical arm candy, and you've lightened your footprint in good soles, there's still the matter of what to put your shopping in.

Have you ever stopped to think how many plastic bags you use in a week? I know that every time I go to the market, even though I take my own bags with me, I still seem to end up with at least three carrier bags filled with spinach or bananas. It just gets exhausting saying no all the time.

On average, each of us throws away 167 plastic carriers every year. Or, to put it another way, each year an estimated 500 billion to one trillion plastic bags are consumed worldwide. That comes out at over one million per minute. The majority will take at least 500 years to decompose in landfill, which really isn't a good thing at all. Billions end up as litter each year, and the consequences can be very nasty: like destroying marine life. Hundreds of thousands of sea turtles, whales and other marine mammals die every year from eating discarded plastic bags mistaken for food.

Some countries have already made progress in eradicating the problem. In 2002, Bangladesh banned them altogether, after it was found they were blocking drainage systems which had contributed to the devastating floods of 1988 and 1998. Demand for jute bags soared. The same year, Ireland introduced the 15 cents per bag PlasTax, which has proved incredibly successful in reducing use by 90 per cent. Quite why plastic bags aren't banned the world over, I don't know. They are horrible things anyway – especially when caught in a tree, waving wildly in the wind for months on end.

But what's the alternative? You might think the answer is paper, but it takes more than four times as much energy to manufacture a paper bag as it does a plastic one. And because most paper comes from tree pulp, it involves cutting down precious trees so they can't even absorb the greenhouse gases created by the manufacture of the bags.

Oh dear, it's one of those no-win situations. I can sympathise with H&M, whose CSR manager confessed that they don't have plans to replace their plastic bags in the near future because the alternatives aren't any better. So the answer is, try to refuse the offer of a plastic bag wherever possible. And make sure you always carry your own 'overspill' bag – preferably made from jute, hemp, or at least unbleached, organic cotton – there are some classic options to choose from.

Bags for life

Waitrose was the first British supermarket to introduce the 'bag for life' concept in 1997. All the major UK supermarkets have followed suit. If you missed the 'I'm Not A Plastic Bag' shopper, Sainsbury's also has a nice jute bag for £1.

For a cooler option, **Howies** has a great 'shop local' jute bag. The jute, grown in West Bengal in India, is very durable and completely biodegradable.

Bags of Change offer a 'stylish sustainable hemp-cotton bag', which acts as a sort of loyalty card to get money off local, Fairtrade and organic goods at participating shops.

Check out **Turtle Bags** for more gorgeous alternatives to plastic bags. The turtle outlasted the dinosaurs, but at the moment it's having trouble outliving us. Scientists examined 473 turtles stranded along the Texas coast between 1983 and 1995. They found ingested plastics in more than half. Turtle Bags use organic and eco-friendly dyes for their string bags (in seventeen colours, including duck egg and pumpkin). They also sell bags made from Indian food sacks (sounds strange, but they're really cool).

If shabby chic is more your thing, you'll love the handmade range at **Carry A Bag**, with logos including 'No More Plastic Bags', 'Dig Your Veg' and 'Mum's Bag', all made from vintage tablecloths and curtains.

Rubbish bags

If you want to get inventive, there are loads of great bags made from recycled materials. Designer **Olga Abadi** uses a cottage industry she has set up in Mexico, employing more than 400 craftsmen to make her quirky bags from scrap materials. Check out www.nahuiollin.com.

Ecoist are a resourceful lot with bags made out of everything from sweet wrappers to film posters and crocheted ring pulls.

They are made in Brazil by women's cooperatives. The company will even plant a tree for every bag sold.

Old textiles from the interiors of vintage cars have proved fertile ground for LA-based designer **Kim White**. Her bags come with a tag giving the year and make of the fabric, so you know exactly what car your bag comes from. She is sold at Harvey Nichols, so you can rest assured she's had approval from the style police.

Designer Allison Teich reduces fashion miles by using a manufacturer in Brooklyn for her brand **AgainNYC**. Her one-off 'junk-to-funk' handbags, clutches and purses are made with serious attention to detail and each one is a gem.

I'm not a plastic bag

Of course a chapter on bags would not be complete without mention of the ultimate bag lady, **Anya Hindmarch**. Collaborating with the wonderful folk at We Are What We Do, Hindmarch got everyone talking plastic in 2007.

When 20,000 of her designer canvas bags went on sale for a fiver a throw at Sainsbury's stores, sane women turned up at 3 a.m. to join the queue. No sooner had the last one sold out, of course, than the backlash began: 'I'm Not an Ethical Bag' screamed the *Evening Standard*'s front page, outraged that the shopper was manufactured in China, using conventional cotton (like they've ever cared before?). Hindmarch says: 'We never claimed this bag is perfect. We have just tried to use our influence as a maker of luxury goods to make it fashionable not to use plastic bags.'

Caring for Your Accessories

How to keep a bag for longer than a season,
By Stuart Vevers, Creative Director at Mulberry

Mulberry uses natural leathers that age over time so the bag becomes more beautiful. The oils from your hands darken the bag, the sunlight changes the leather and it all adds to their heirloom quality. I design them to have longevity, partly due to some of the retro styling.

Every season, it gets more difficult to name a bag. We don't name them until right at the end. Some seasons, we go for feminine names, others it might be more retro so we go for an old-fashioned name (this season it's the Mabel) or places. We spend quite a lot of time deciding. If you get it wrong it stays with you.

People do buy a bag for a season, but there are also those who want their bag to last for years. Mulberry has a repair service and it is well used. You get bags from twenty years ago that someone has really loved and can't bear to part with. It creates a loyal customer.

To keep your bag in the best condition, there are sprays for leather to avoid water marking and nourishers to look after the leather.

Leather likes warm temperatures and when you pack a bag away, stuff it with paper and keep out the light.

Confessions of a bag lady
by Anya Hindmarch

Just to show that she has nothing to hide – and that she has never pretended to be without fault – Anya Hindmarch let us have a peek into her working wardrobe to see how she tries to dress well, but with a conscience:

* I buy what I need and wear it to death.
* I tend to buy five outfits for a season, and then either sell on, archive or donate them to Oxfam. I am quite ruthless.
* I tend to allow myself probably three, day bags per season, which I will rotate. I feel a bit guilty having too many things, but I love the three I choose and hand them on to my daughters afterwards, so they do get recycled.
* In truth, I probably only wear 50 per cent of my wardrobe.
* I buy my underwear and cotton basics from websites – www.figleaves.com and www.shopbop.com mainly – James Pearce is great for cotton basics.

* I think that supermarkets and high street shops do great fashion and Topshop is wonderful. But the clothes don't last as long.
* I mend my clothes. Sew buttons, darn them, patch children's jeans – all that stuff.
* The oldest thing in my wardrobe would be something from my mother – an old black opera coat from the 1970s. I love it.
* I buy a lot of vintage clothes. I think it's fun to wear something that is a one-off, so it's a fashion issue.
* I have a fur jacket, which I sometimes feel a little unsure about. I almost wore it to launch the plastic bag shopper, but thought, I can't be launching an eco bag in that! It's made of rabbit and rabbit is eaten.

How to make your shoes last forever
By Georgina Goodman, designer

* I've got shoes that are twenty years old – I'm a real hoarder. My favourites are a pair of purple thigh-length boots from Patrick Cox that I bought in the King's Road in the 1980s (showing my age!)
* I am really hard on shoes – if I find a pair I like wearing, I'll wear them into the ground. This is the worst thing you can do to a pair of shoes.
* To make your shoes last, rotate your shoe wardrobe.
* Don't dry leather soles near heat.
* Keep your shoes in boxes.
* Don't let your heel tips wear down – replace before you wreck the heels.
* Buy great shoes – the better the quality, the longer they will last.

Finding a really good cobbler is my best tip for keeping your shoes forever. Try Hugh Greenly (www.hughgreenly.co.uk) who has been cobbling away for over sixty years and could, I imagine, repair and save any pair of shoes you sent his way. He offers a mail order service.

You get what you pay for, and if you are in the market for a pair of classic brogues or Oxfords, invest in Trickers, Grensons or one of the other great British manufacturers, who still offer their own repair service, which means that these really are shoes for life.

Last but not Least . . .

If you are green and sporty (girl, how virtuous can you get!)

Remember to recycle your trainers. One of the worst footwear offenders in terms of landfill is the trainer. Even the simplest sports shoe can use more than ten different materials, making it impossible to biodegrade – just think of all those high-tech synthetic nasties sitting in a hole in the ground and not going anywhere fast. Use Nike's Reuse-A-Shoe scheme for disposing of unwanted trainers (they don't even have to be Nike). If they are good enough to still be worn, they will be redistributed. If they are simply too smelly/at the end of their life (serious runners should change their trainers every 300 miles or so – I'd be lucky if I walk that in a lifetime) the shoes are sliced and ground up into a material they like to call Nike Grind, which is used to make surfaces for sports and playgrounds.

Oxfam, Traid, the Salvation Army and most charity shops will accept all second-hand shoes. If they are still wearable, they will get a second life.

If you prefer your trainers a little less corporate, there are a few great ethical trainer specialists, including Veja, No Sweat and Worn Again.

See the Little Green Book for details on all the bags and shoes mentioned in this chapter.

10

All that Glitters

All that Glitters

'Gold cannot be pure, and people cannot be perfect'

Chinese proverb

A Girl's Best Friend?

Mention ethical jewellery, and I do admit you get a certain sinking feeling. Experience teaches us not to get excited: it's brown, it's clunky, it's wooden beads, shells, ethnic carving . . . It's going to look like you bought it at Oxfam. Now there is no reason why Oxfam's Fairtrade jewellery has to look the way it does – all carved gourd bangles and Balinese hoops, a bit too 'ethnic' and worthy for its own good. And while Traidcraft is doing a great job promoting fair trade, its products could benefit from a freshen up.

None of us can resist a bit of sparkle. Whether we lust after diamonds or pearls, gold, silver, or even plastic beads, it's the finishing touch that makes a look. Happily, I can report that 'green jewellery' has undergone something of a makeover recently. I'm not a big jewellery wearer, but I have been seduced by many of the collections I have seen while researching this chapter, particularly some of the pieces that make use of recycled materials. Somehow, resourcefulness breeds creativity.

I love the way jewellery can be made out of literally anything, even an old flip-flop washed up on a beach. **Tanvi Kant** (www.tanvi kant.co.uk) makes the most beautiful, simple forms by binding, knotting and winding scraps of old fabric to make bracelets and necklaces. She was inspired by the hand-stitched hem of her mother's silk sari and loves the idea of recycling material. She will even make a piece especially for you if you have a bit of fabric or an old item of clothing you are particularly attached to.

The possibilities with ethical jewellery are endlessly inspiring – especially when you find out how easy it is to make your own. And this is great news, because traditional gems are fast losing their lustre. It's hard to see the beauty in something once you find out that its origins are ugly. As eco jewellery designer to the stars, **Pippa Small**, points out, 'Jewellery is not like coffee, bananas or jeans. At least they all have a function. Jewellery is the one thing that is useless, and in a way that's why it's so important that it is ethically sourced. Do you want to wear a ring that someone has died over or that has caused rivers to be polluted?'

For the love of diamonds

Leonardo DiCaprio's film *Blood Diamond* really got people talking about the realities of the diamond trade – and in particular, the shocking business of conflict diamonds, where stones are illegally traded for arms, contributing to devastating conflicts in Angola, the Democratic Republic of the Congo, Sierra Leone and other African countries.

The Kimberley Process (www.kimberleyprocess.com), a joint government, industry and civil society initiative, was set up in 2003 to ensure that blood diamonds were blocked from the market. According to the industry's official World Diamond Council it's had great success – conflict stones have reportedly been reduced to less than 1 per cent. But organisations such as Global Witness, Survival International and Conflict Neutral, which monitor the diamond trade, point out that it is still impossible to trace any individual cut diamond, and consequently to be certain whether a diamond is conflict free. And 1 per cent is still significant.

Unfortunately, the whole business of diamond dealing and accreditation – particularly of polished stones – has no independent verification or enforcement systems. So if you're looking for an ethical diamond, it's not easy.

One idea is to seek out Canadian diamonds. Canada was the first mining industry in the world to develop and adopt an environmental policy. In a business that is so lucrative, miners elsewhere work in poor and dangerous conditions and with very low pay. Fair trade has yet to come into it.

There are a select number of jewellery companies that strive to be completely ethical. **Dejoria**, for one, 'is prepared to guarantee that every diamond sold is conflict free'. If hip-hop, big bling is your sort of thing, check out the **Green Initiative Collection** by yoga-loving Russell Simmons and his wife, Kimora Lee. They already make the sort of jewels that have your eyes popping out of their sockets. And 25 per cent of the price of every piece in this collection goes to the Diamond Empowerment Fund, raising money for the education, health and development of communities in Africa. Beyoncé Knowles, Eddie Murphy and Penelope Cruz are already wearing theirs.

Ed Zwick, the producer of *Blood Diamond*, spent two years researching the industry and has called for it 'to dedicate a portion of every single African diamond sale to the rebuilding of infrastructure and the creation of sustainable development'. This would be the equivalent of the (Product) Red campaign for diamonds. Let's hope it happens soon.

Good as gold?

It's not just diamonds that are a problem. Extracting gold is a dirty business too, harmful both to those who mine and purify it, and to the environment. Cyanide and mercury are commonly used to separate gold, poisoning the miners and the earth.

Pippa Small, the jeweller beloved by the likes of Julia Roberts, Cameron Diaz, Saffron Burrows and Mick Jagger, is in the process of setting up a relationship with a Bolivian mine to use 'clean' gold. And designer Greg Valerio of **Cred** travelled from gentle West Sussex to Chocó, Colombia, in search of pure gold to make wedding rings. Cred knows for sure now that its gold is mined responsibly and without exploitation. It is refined using hydrogen peroxide rather than the noxious nitric acid, and the land is reforested after use.

Valerio's company has also collaborated with Katharine Hamnett, who is truly fired-up about the issue. 'Do you know about it?' she asks. 'They crush the rocks and then they use thousands of tonnes of cyanide which actually leaches the gold out. And in another process they use mercury if they have a slurry, and then children get the gold at the bottom. Cyanide leaches into the river, and anything downstream. Look at the mercury levels in the fish: it's permanent poisoning! Most of our gold (and silver) is mined that way. A gold ring causes environmental devastation across the planet. They say that one wedding ring creates three tonnes of toxic waste, possibly as much as 120 tonnes for a massive rapper's chain. It's environmental lawlessness and a complete disregard for human rights!' I can feel another T-shirt coming on . . .

The selection of rings designed by Hamnett for Cred uses gold mined by a cooperative using ancient techniques. As Hamnett explains, 'They find a bend in the river with a sinuvial deposit, and they mine it for two years, cut down all the trees and it ends up like a ziggurat. After two years, they fill it in, replant the indigenous trees and leave it in a better state than they found it. It's good! They get a premium and we put in a percentage of our profits. We did that because we want to highlight the situation.'

It's worth noting that the Fairtrade foundation are looking into developing a mark for sustainable, ethically mined gold, so it won't be long before you can see at a glance if your gold really is worth its weight.

A Brighter Future?

Have you ever stopped to think about where, or rather who made your glass bead earrings and your matching necklace? These days, it's so easy to pick up a bright new bangle for a few pounds. Unfortunately, chances are it was made in the Far East or India, using child labour. Little hands make light work of fiddly little things. The cheaper the trinket, the more likely that it has been made by kids who work 10-12 hours a day to send £4 a month to their families back home – or that it was made in a sweatshop.

Thankfully, there are alternatives – and good ones too. Fair Trade companies like **People Tree** work with adults who are paid a decent wage (which means their children don't have to work). A necklace made out of horn beads helps to fund People Tree's Sports For All campaign, providing sporting activities for disadvantaged children in Delhi.

Made – fairly and squarely

Cristina Cisilino has vision. She set up her Fair Trade company, **Made**, in 2005, with the aim of producing great, cutting-edge accessories. Determined to incorporate fair trade principles into her business, she decided to cut out the middlemen and deal with the makers direct. And as if this wasn't smart enough, she also enlisted the help of some great designers, including Olivia Morris (shoes), and Sam Ubhi and Pippa Small (jewellery), who were happy to contribute their time and expertise for free.

In Kenya, a country where a copy of *Vogue* costs the equivalent of six months' wages, a little design input is necessary to give the makers the edge on their competitors. By casting a design eye on the accessories that were already being produced, Made have created a collection that has the vibrancy and energy of its makers, together with a contemporary Western twist. It's selling out as fast as Topshop can stock it. And I'd wager that's not because it is helping improve the lives of those who make it, but because the pieces are gorgeously seductive.

When I quizzed Cristina, her bestseller was a bracelet made from seeds, probably beaded by Moses, a Maasai who has a way with intricate beadwork. Before he met Cristina, Moses was making key-rings and selling them from a stall in the slums of Kibera. Now he has a makeshift workroom and is making a relatively decent living as a key member of Cristina's team.

Cristina also recycles some of the waste that is washed up on the streets and beaches of Africa. So far she's managed to create beauty from plastic bags, driftwood, bones, seeds, recycled bottles and even bullets (a tragic by-product of the war in Sudan, these can be melted down into aluminium). One of her most ingenious raw materials is the industrial quantity of flip-flops that are coming on to the beaches of Tanzania and Kenya, on the east coast of Africa. She was alerted to the flip-flop influx by a biologist working to protect the reefs. So Cristina sends someone to collect them every day, and they are made into necklaces. In the poorest regions of the world, everything has a value and a use. The first batches sold out of Oxford Street within days.

Tatty Devine

In east London too, one man's junk is another man's treasure. For Harriet Vine and Rosie Wolfenden, two friends who met studying Fine Art at Chelsea School of Art in 1996, a chance encounter with a row of bin-bags outside an upholstery shop led to them starting their own jewellery company, **Tatty Devine**. Never pass a bin-bag or a skip without a quick peek inside. You never know what you might find!

The fourteen bin-bags they found were packed with sample books, and they couldn't resist carting them off home. They'd had a few drinks at the pub, after all. Harriet made a cuff and an old hair slide, which friends commented on, so she decided to dig out the sample books and make some more. Since then, they've used all manner of unlikely materials to make their jewels. They've used cake decorations for charm bracelets and old key-rings for belts; they've threaded toy cars on to necklaces and used toys from crackers, plectrums, tape measures, chess pieces and poker chips. They've even carved wooden owl pendants out of old mahogany floorboards. All their jewellery is made in their studio in east London, round the corner from their shop, so they employ local people and buy their raw materials locally too. Here are their tips on how to create your own treasures.

How to make your own junky jewellery
By Tatty Devine

* Take old necklaces apart and rethread them. Clasps can be bought easily in craft shops, or use ribbons (left from Christmas and birthday presents).

* Make papier-mâché beads out of old news or wrapping paper.

* Cracker toys can make good charms or pendants. I got a red plastic mirror in the shape of a hand that I wear as a necklace.

* Old horse brasses make good pendants.

* We like safety-pin jewellery, or paperclips, anything that you can attach together.

* Old glasses from charity shops – take the lenses out, snap arms off and put on a ribbon . . . your very own Tatty Devine-style glasses necklace!

* Old key-rings bunched together on a cord. It's a good look to collect loads of things and put them on a chain or cord. The brighter the better.

* An easy and effective way to make a bead necklace is to get a long strip of fabric, and sew it lengthways into a tube. Get something to stuff it with (even cotton wool would do). Tie a knot in one end, put a little stuffing in, then pull a bead on, then more stuffing, then another bead and so on, until you have fabric bead followed by a real bead. This can be done up with a safety pin or ribbon or clasps from a haberdashery.

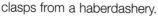

The power of hands

In the aftermath of the 2004 Indian Ocean tsunami, Andrea Galer's foundation, the **Power of Hands**, was set up to help the Sri Lankan lacemakers whose lives had been devastated. Sri Lanka has long been famous for its crafts, and the lacemakers of Galle, in the south of the country, have been spinning their magic ever since the Portuguese introduced the skill in the fifteenth century. A costume designer by trade, Andrea has used the lace for the costumes in the Jane Austen film *Persuasion*. You can order the exquisite accessories online – including Lily Cole's favourite lace bracelets – at www.powerofhandsfoundation.org

●★◉★

Precious things

Pippa Small is another top-rate designer, transforming fashion and livelihoods with her gorgeous jewellery. Movie stars and fashion editors covet her chunky 'clean' gold and uncut crystal rings. And her recycled brass bracelets and necklaces for Made have been a huge hit – and a great way of buying into a more affordable side of her work.

Small spends half her professional life as an anthropologist. For years, she has been working with indigenous tribes, like the Kuna Indians, who live in Kuna Yale, a small territory of rainforest and coral islands off the coast of Panama (and whom she first encountered, wearing gold from head to toe).

Developing local crafts and paying fair prices are integral to her work. 'In some isolated groups, they have absolutely no sense of money,' she says. 'You could pay 1p or £100, which is why there has been terrible exploitation.'

Her designs enable tribespeople to rediscover value in their work and resurrect some of the old skills that might otherwise be lost. Working with the Kuna, she says, 'I went round to all the grandmothers, pulled out their jewellery and discussed why it was more beautiful because it was imperfect and wonky and handmade.' The results are truly stunning, and you can buy them online at www.pippasmall.com.

The Greenest Gems

The greenest gem is in fact blue . . . I have seen a glorious blue tanzanite ring in a Bond Street jewellers and it has all the bling factor – and more – of the shiniest sapphire. Discovered in 1967, apparently by a Maasai tribesman called Ali Juuywatu, tanzanite occurs in only one part of the world: the foothills of Mount Kilimanjaro in Tanzania (hence the name). Because of this, it is preciously guarded and its mines can be closely regulated.

The tanzanite industry has a commitment to ethical business practices, environmentally responsible mining practices, and reinvestment in the local community. It is one of the few precious gemstones whose supply chain is fairly transparent and easy to trace. The industry is supported by the Tanzanite Foundation, a not-for-profit organisation that helps market the stone, and also helps support other sustainable projects.

The beauty of recycled glass

Who hasn't wandered along a beach and picked up a piece of luminous green glass, polished by the waves, and pretended it's an emerald? I usually come back from trips to the seaside with pockets full of treasure. It's amazing what you can find on a beachcombing trip, and there's something comforting about a smooth pebble to play with in your pocket. Hold it up to the light, and you are instantly transported to the seaside. I end up carrying mine around for ages.

Jewellery designer Gina Cowen was inspired to work with sea-glass following a walk along a stretch of shingle near Cape Town, where she was born. Finding the beach scattered with pale, frosted sapphires, emeralds, amber and crystal, transformed broken bottles from the nearby harbour pub, she collected a handful of these sea-tumbled gems to make her first necklace, drilling the glass pebbles to form a collar of light. These days she finds most of the treasure for her company **Sea Glass Jewellery** on British shores, including one beach where the tides still bring up multi-coloured delights, remnants from a Victorian glass factory.

Slightly less romantic, but almost as fabulous, is jewellery made from recycled bottles. The colours are clear, and the beads are so smooth. Glass bottles are in plentiful supply, of course, and the Cornish company **Green Glass** gets through thousands of them a week, making really simple but sumptuous bracelets and necklaces in bright blues and greens. The company's processes are designed to be as energy efficient as possible and they filter and reuse all the water in their factory. But the beads are the star of the show. Pile on a few at a time for maximum effect.

As you've seen, there are so many brilliantly inventive and creative things being done with jewellery, but perhaps one of the most worthwhile (and spectacular) ventures is that of the Bushmen of Botswana. As she started this book so eloquently, I would like to give Lily Cole the last word, on the Traid Not Aid project she fell in love with:

Treading on eggshells
By Lily Cole

66 Ostrich egg jewellery is some of the most beautiful I've ever seen. In a market where most products have lost that human connection between creation and product, I think anything that is handmade is wonderful. But this jewellery is particularly exquisite. Botswana Bushmen use nail clippers to painstakingly fashion beads out of ostrich eggshells. Then they string them together.

You can still smell the fires they've been made next to; you can almost feel each bead's story in their beautifully uneven texture. Each piece takes months of hand labour to craft, which I've seen first hand. These pieces are unlike anything else you will find on the market, and I can't think of any group of economically marginalised people I'd rather give my money to in exchange for owning something beautiful and unique. 99

For more information email Birthe Gjern at gantsicraft@botsnet.bw

Tamsin Blanchard
Silkworm Farm
Green Street
London

Dear Sir

I recently bought a lovely print dress from your Oxford Street shop I am enjoying wearing it and it has attracted lots of compliments but I am feeling a little guilty that it only cost £12.99. I noticed that the label says it is made i

11

Little Green Book

Little Green Book

'Just remember, if the world didn't suck, we'd all fall off'

Anonymous

Stylish and Sustainable Shopping Directory

Key to symbols

 vintage

 fair trade

 recycled

 organic

 vegetarian

 craft

Absolute Vintage
Quality vintage clothing and accessories from the 1930s to 1980s, including the largest selection of shoes in the UK.
www.absolutevintage.co.uk

Adili
The ultimate one-stop, ethical fashion shop, stocks all our favourite brands from Patagonia to Stewart & Brown.
www.adili.com

AgainNYC
Allison Teich's fantastic handbags, clutches and purses are made using textiles produced locally to the designer.
www.againnyc.com

Amana
Well-edited, well-designed working girl's wardrobe, made by women artisans in the Middle Atlas Mountains, Morocco, using sustainable fabrics.
www.amana-collection.com

Bill Amberg
The ultimate in high-quality vege-tanned leather.
www.billamberg.com

American Apparel
Sweat-shop free streetwear in all the colours of the rainbow.
www.americanapparel.net

Anya Hindmarch
Hindmarch teamed up with social change movement We Are What We Do to create the It Bag of 2007. Check the site for details on how to get your own 'I'm Not a Plastic Bag'.
www.anyahindmarch.com

Ascension
100 per cent organic jeans with fair trade certification. All

profits from Ascension sales go directly to build schools, orphanages and health centres in India.
www.ascensionclothing.co.uk

Bags of Change
For stylish, original alternatives to a plastic bag.
www.bagsofchange.co.uk

Bamboo Clothes
Sustainable clothing from spun bamboo – it's the new cotton, don't you know?
www.bambooclothes.com

Beyond Retro
An Aladdin's cave for vintage fans – rails are arranged by decade and, from Edwardian ballgowns to a 60s suit made from popcorn, they have everything.
www.beyondretro.com

Beyond Skin
Handmade vegetarian shoes, as worn by Natalie Portman.
www.beyondskin.co.uk

Biome
Australian-based company making green living easy: eco-friendly gifts, toxin-free natural home skincare, organic bed linen, and more.
www.biome.com.au

Carry A Bag
Handmade, shabby chic bags – you'll never use plastic again.
www.carry-a-bag.com

Charmone Shoes
American, cruelty-free shoes pioneers.
www.charmoneshoes.com

Ciel

Organic, environmentally and ethically produced, and very, very beautiful – Sarah Ratty's award-winning label continually raises the bar for eco-fashion.
www.ciel.ltd.uk

Clothes Swap

For your nearest clothes swap in the UK.
www.clothesswap.meetup.com

Cred

Greg Valerio's fair trade jewellery company, with a heart of pure gold.
www.cred.tv

Dejoria

Ethical jewellery company that 'guarantees conflict-free diamonds'.
www.dejoria.co.uk

Del-forte

Fabulous, organic jeans, including great shapes: high waist, skinny, and shorts.
www.delforte.com

Draper's Organic

For a great selection of hemp rucksacks.
www.drapersorganiccotton.co.uk

Earth Tote Bags

Organic cotton, hemp shopping bags, backpacks and sling bags, from Australia.
www.earthtotebags.com.au

Eco Boudoir
Sexy, luxurious and environmentally friendly – check out the bamboo silk lingerie and home furnishings.
www.eco-boudoir.com

Eco-labels
Consumers Union website, providing a helpful guide to environmental labels.
www.eco-labels.org

Ecoist
Colourful bags and belts made in Brazil, from recycled materials.
www.ecoist.com

Edun
Stylish clothing from Ali Hewson, Bono and Rogan Gregory, supporting Africa and the developing world.
www.edunonline.com

Enamore
Check out the vintage style, organic hemp and silk underwear and pretty summer dresses.
www.enamore.co.uk

Equa Clothing
Pioneering ethical clothing boutique – great for People Tree, Ciel and Enamore, plus all the latest cutting-edge eco fashion.
www.equaclothing.com

Ethical Superstore
Huge range of eco-friendly and fair trade clothes, including the bestselling brands and the very latest products.
www.ethicalsuperstore.com

Freitag
Cycling fans will love their recycled messenger bag.
www.freitag.ch

From Somewhere
Orsola de Castro recycles the waste from big designers to make beautiful, timeless pieces. This is recycling at its most luxurious.
www.fromsomewhere.co.uk

Funkifish
Quirky cool, 'aqua-leather' bags and accessories, tanned from fish skins.
www.funkifish.com

Gecoz
Australian store with scrumptious bedding, clothes, skincare products and lots more.
www.gecoz.net.au

Gominyc
New York's coolest, eco-boutique – great for hot, fashion-forward looks that you can rely on to be environmentally and ethically friendly.
www.gominyc.com

Goodone
One-off clothes, made from hand-picked, recycled fabrics.
www.goodone.co.uk

Gossypium
Affordable ethical clothing made from sustainable materials – a great place to shop for Fairtrade, organic cotton.
www.gossypium.co.uk

Got Soul
Australian Mecca for all things environmentally friendly, cruelty-free and vegan.
www.gotsoul.com.au

Green Baby
Environmentally sound, sustainable shop for babies – everything from clothes to cots.
www.greenbaby.co.uk

Green Fibres
Great basics and underwear in organic cotton and hemp.
www.greenfibres.com

Green Glass
From funky glasses to jewellery – all made from recycled glass.
www.greenglass.co.uk

Ethical Superstore
Everything you could want online from Fairtrade wine to eco kettles.
www.ethicalsuperstore.com

Green Knickers
Pretty, witty smalls for those who care about big issues: seduce in the silk/hemp mix, or make a statement with the 'eat organic' limited edition design.
www.greenknickers.org

Green Weddings
Ruth Culver is the wedding planner to contact for your dream day. For when green is the new white …
www.greenweddings.org.uk

Howies

Organic cotton clothing with a cult following. Cool, surfy vibe, great policies.

www.howies.co.uk

Hug

Lovely, simple, fairly traded – great for your wardrobe basics.

www.hug.co.uk

James Jeans

American-style denim made using an organic compound.

www.jamesjeans.us

Junky Styling

London's premier recycled clothing company can deconstruct and reconstruct virtually anything. Don't forget to visit their Wardrobe Surgery service.

www.junkystyling.co.uk

Karen Cole

Natural, cruelty-free knitwear, using New Zealand Merino wool.

www.karencole.co.uk

Katharine E Hamnett

The first place to go for your 100 per cent organic, fairly traded, slogan T-shirts, plus clothes that are eco but don't look it.

www.katharinehamnett.com

Kika & Ferret

Get in the holiday spirit in the best kikois this side of Kenya.

www.kicaandferret.com

Kim White
This LA designer makes brilliant, incredibly durable bags from vintage car fabrics.
www.kimwhitehandbags.com

Kuyichi
Brilliantly directional, style-conscious denim – as stocked in Topshop.
www.kuyichi.com

Linda Loudermilk
LA's favourite for red carpet glamour, quirky style and sustainable fabrics.
www.lindaloudermilk.com

Loomstate
Rogan Gregory's 100 per cent organic jeans will win you serious credibility – even with denim anoraks.
www.loomstate.org

Lovelylovely
Extremely pretty, cheeky and original range of fashion tableware and accessories.
www.lovelylovely.net

Made
The brainchild of Cristina Cisilino, this is gorgeous fair trade jewellery, made 'by the people for the people', and selling fast at Topshop.
www.made.uk.com

Maison de la Fausse Fourrure
This French boutique is the place to go for fake fur.
www.maisondelafaussefourrure.com

Matt & Nat

Quirky, cruelty-free bags that come with a 'positivity message' inside.
www.mattandnat.com

The Natural Store

Stocks all the best eco-brands, and a huge range of products, from clothing to travel and leisure: an inspiring, easy place to shop online.
www.thenaturalstore.co.uk

No Sweat

Sweatshop-free range of American casual clothing and footwear.
www.nosweatapparel.com

Noir

Classy, edgy designs using organic fabrics and interesting finishes.
www.noir-illuminati2.com

Oasis

Oasis's Future Organic collection is a denim and T-shirt range made using 100% organic denim and jersey, which is – as the name correctly says – the future.
www. oasis-stores.com

Ollie & Nic

Great non-leather bags made from corduroy, hessian and other eco-materials.
www.ollieandnic.com

Patagonia

Ethical clothing for active people. Get your cycling gear here – and recycle your longjohns and T-shirts while you're at it.
www.patagonia.com

People Tree
The conscientious fashionista's choice: fabulous, ethical and selling out fast in Topshop.
www.peopletree.co.uk

Pippa Small
Unique, ethical jewellery, beloved by fashion editors and movie stars alike. See also her affordable collection for Made.
www.pippasmall.com

Planet Truth
Australian company that supports sustainable agriculture and local designers: cracking range of urban organic T-shirts too.
www.planet-truth.com

Product Red
The brand co-created by Bono to raise awareness and money for the Global Fund. A portion of profits go towards helping AIDS victims in Africa. Companies involved include Converse, Gap, Giorgio Armani, Motorola, American Express and Apple.
www.joinred.com

Rally
100 per cent Australian-made and certified organic cotton T-shirt collection.
www.rallyclothing.com.au

Rellik
London's premier vintage boutique, stocking clothing from the 1920s to mid 1980s, and designers including Vivienne Westwood, Christian Dior and Pucci.
www.relliklondon.co.uk

Sea Glass Jewellery
Spoils from the sea, reinvented by designer Gina Cowen.
www.seaglass.co.uk

Shoefolk
Ethically sourced vegetable tanned leather.
www.shoefolk.com

Slow and Steady Wins the Race
Mary Ping's brilliant counterculture fashion and accessories
line – fantastic for bags.
www.slowandsteadywinstherace.com

Steinberg & Tolkien
An Aladdin's cave of antique designer costume jewellery,
vintage and contemporary clothing and accessories. No
website as yet.
193 Kings Road, Chelsea, SW3 5EB

Stella McCartney
Funky, fabulous, needs no introduction – for when you want
chic, ethical and kind.
www.stellamccartney.com

Stewart & Brown
Feminine dresses and knits including Mongolian cashmere,
made from sustainable materials. One per cent of profit is
given back to environmental causes.
www.stewartbrown.com

Tatty Bumpkin
Organic and ethically sourced clothing for kids.
www.tattybumpkin.com

Tatty Devine
Highly creative online boutique, for unique and quirky accessories.
www.tattydevine.com

Terra Plana
Fashion-conscious, sustainable streetwear and shoes.
www.terraplana.com

Traid Remade
Charity shop label, transforming unloved cast-offs into fantastic new one-off designs.
www.traid.org.uk

Turtle bags
Gorgeous alternative to plastic bags – eco-friendly dyes and organic materials used.
www.turtlebags.co.uk

V V Rouleaux
Haberdashery in London with the best selection of beads, ribbons and trimmings.
www.vvrouleaux.com

Wildlife Works
Environmentally friendly 'products as good for the planet as they are for your soul', designed to finance wildlife conservation in Kenya.
www.wildlifeworks.com

Worn Again
Cracking trainers made from recycled material.
www.wornagain.co.uk

Health and beauty

✳ **Aubrey Organics**
Hair, skin and body care, using herbals, essential oils and natural vitamins.
www.aubrey-organics.com

✳ **Avea**
One stop organic beauty shop.
www.avea.co.uk

✳ **Aveda**
Leading brand in organic hair and beauty products.
www.aveda.com

✳ **The Alchemist's Apprentice**
Organic beauty products, as favoured by Charlize Theron.
www.alchemistsapprentice.com

✳ **Balm Balm**
Winner of the 2007 Best Organic Beauty Award, sponsored by the Soil Association – great face and lip balms.
www.balmbalm.com

✳ **Dr Hauschka**
The independent, natural organic beauty firm that Stella McCartney recommends. They even do a line in vegan brushes.
www.drhauschka.co.uk

Green People
Check out the organic Red Shimmer lipstick.
www.greenpeople.co.uk

✳ **The Organic Pharmacy**
Online pharmacy, dedicated to organic health and beauty products and treatments.
www.theorganicpharmacy.com

Other great, organic natural beauty and health sites include:

www.beingorganic.com

www.burtsbees.com

www.cargoplantlove.com

www.drbronner.com

www.ecolani.com

www.lavera.co.uk

www.lizearle.com

www.nealsyardremedies.com

www.origins.co.uk

www.soorganic.com

www.stellamccartneycare.com

www.theremustbeabetterway.co.uk

www.trevarnoskincare.co.uk

www.victoriahealth.com

www.weleda.co.uk

Fun things to do

 Canvas Chic
Luxury yurt holidays.
www.canvaschic.com

Cast Off
Join the knitting revolution at Cast Off club's sociable, online home.
www.castoff.info

Happy Campers
Kat and Tess inspire with the joys of camping – food, fun, freedom and food for the soul. Includes 'the really good campsite guide', for best spots around the UK.
www.thehappycampers.co.uk

Just Green
If you fancy joining me and starting your own silkworm farm, Just Green is the supplier I'd recommend.
www.just-green.com

Queens of Noize
For folking-it-up nights that let you get back to your hippy roots, and stay in fashion.
www.queensofnoize.com

RSA Carbon Limited
This user-friendly carbon counter will enable you to work out your own footprint and how to reduce it.
www.rsacarbonlimited.org

Responsible Travel
Plenty of answers on how to enjoy responsible travel.
www.responsibletravel.com

Stitch 'n' Bitch

Get creative and meet others who enjoy the joy of knitting. The site will help you find a local network, or use its handy guide to start your own Knit and Natter network.
www.stitchnbitch.co.uk

Supernaturale

Be inspired by this independent US site, 'dedicated to Do It Yourself culture in all its glorious forms'.
www.supernaturale.com

Walk It

For thinking outside the Tube . . . the best routes to walk around London, and a guide to how much carbon pollution you have saved.
www.walkit.com

Wellbeing Escapes

Search for the rare, the best kept secret, and the ultimate stress-free escapes – from yoga in the Himalayas to a day in a top spa in London.
www.wellbeingescapes.co.uk

Green Reads

Books

A Slice of Organic Life: Get Closer to the Soil Without Going the Whole Hog by Sheherazade Goldsmith

The Cheap Date Guide to Style by Kira Jolliffe and Bay Garnett

Cradle to Cradle: Remaking the Way We Make Things by William McDonough

Glamorous Movie Stars of the Fifties Paper Dolls by Tom Tierney

The Happy Campers by Kat Heyes and Tess Carr

Hookorama: 25 Fabulous Things to Crochet, (Paperback) by Rachael Matthews

How to Save the World Without Really Trying, The Idler Issue 38 (Green Man) by Tom Hodgkinson

Heat: How to Stop the Planet Burning by George Monbiot

In Praise of Slow: How a Worldwide Movement is Challenging the Cult of Speed by Carl Honore

It's Vintage, Darling! How to be a Clothes Connoisseur by Christa Weil

Knitorama: 25 Great & Glam Things to Knit by Rachael Matthews

Knitting With Dog Hair: Better A Sweater From A Dog You Know and Love Than From A Sheep You'll Never Meet by Kendall Crolius

Make Do and Mend by Hugh Dalton

Making Vintage Bags: 20 Original Sewing Patterns for Vintage Bags and Purses by Emma Brennan

No Logo by Naomi Klein

Not Buying It: My Year Without Shopping by Judi Levine

Organic Cotton from Field to Final Product edited by Dorothy Myers and Sue Stolton

Shopped: The Shocking Power of British Supermarkets by Joanna Blythman

Yeah! I Made it Myself by Eithne Farry

Magazines and websites

Anti-Apathy
Guaranteed to spur you into action. Check out the '10 Easy Steps to Reduce your Ecological Footprint'.
www.antiapathy.org

The Ecologist
Environmental affairs magazine that covers everything to do with ethical issues.
www.theecologist.org

Ecorazzi
Celebrity gossip with an eco edge.
www.ecorazzi.com

The Environmental Justice Foundation
Pick your cotton carefully – read the information on this website. It inspired Lily Cole to do more, and Katharine Hamnett to design her 'Save the Future' T-shirt.
www.ejfoundation.org

The Ethical Consumer
UK alternative consumer magazine.
www.ethicalconsumer.org

The Fairtrade Foundation
Includes a comprehensive list of all the certified Fairtrade cotton brands.
www.fairtrade.org.uk

Global Cool
Stellar ideas to help save the planet – supported by the likes of Josh Hartnett, Kate Bosworth, Pink, Razorlight, The Killers and Sugababes.
www.global-cool.com

The Green Guide
National Geographic website on how to be green.
www.thegreenguide.com

Grist
Eco news and comment.
www.grist.org

Labour Behind the Label
Vital campaign to improve working conditions worldwide – read
the report 'Who Pays for Cheap Clothes?' from July 2006.
www.labourbehindthelabel.org

New Consumer
The UK's leading ethical lifestyle magazine, with inspiring fashion
features.
www.newconsumer.com

Pesticide Action Network
Everything you need to know about organic cotton and the
dangers of pesticides.
www.pan.uk.org

Reusable Bags
For endless information on the evils of plastic – and some useful
solutions.
www.reusablebags.com

Style Will Save Us
Fashionable green lifestyle online magazine.
www.stylewillsaveus.com

Sublime
Stylish magazine on all aspects of an ethical lifestyle.
www.sublimemagazine.com

Treehugger
Online eco-bible, featuring in-depth sections on all aspects of

ethical living.
www.treehugger.com

War on Want
Read the report 'Fashion Victims: The True Cost of Cheap Clothes at Primark, Asda and Tesco'. Chastening, but necessary stuff.
www.waronwant.org

Green Letter Day

Writing a letter not only allows you to get things off your chest, it's a really effective way of making change happen. If you take the time to handwrite a well-crafted letter, chances are someone will read it, file it, take note, and – you never know – even write back.

Now is a great time to get writing because companies are looking at ways to change, and a little bit of extra encouragement from you (and you, and you!) may spur them on to just go that bit further.

The main issues worth writing about are:

1. Working conditions, to make it clear to our favourite shops that we love their clothes, but we don't love the idea of people being treated unfairly or exploited along the way. We want to shop. We want to spend our money. But we want to know that the money – and enough of it – is going to the right places. Ask about fair trade clothes and accessories.

2. Pesticides and chemicals. Cotton grown using pesticides is a no-win situation. As more companies are producing organic cotton collections, write to them to let them know you approve, and tell them you want to be able to buy all their clothes in organic cotton. If your favourite brand is not using organic cotton, write to them and ask why not?

Here, to help you on your way, are two letter templates to amend and send. The first questions working conditions and the second is designed to encourage the high street – or your favourite designer – to go organic. Either copy them out in your best handwriting, or use them as a basis for your own heartfelt plea.

Is it fair?

Dear Sir,

I recently bought a lovely print dress from your Oxford Street shop. I am enjoying wearing it, and it has attracted lots of compliments, but I am feeling a little guilty that it only cost £12.99. I noticed that the label doesn't actually say where it was made, and I am writing to ask for information about the working conditions in the factories that produce this dress.

I am a regular customer (please see enclosed receipt) but I would like to know that the clothes I am buying are made in decent conditions and that the workers who produce my clothes are treated fairly. I wonder how much of my £12.99 is paid to the person who made it?

I couldn't find any information on your website about these policies so I would be interested to hear about any work you are doing on these issues. Do you have a code of conduct or an ethical policy, and do you audit your factories for working conditions? What evidence can you send me of working conditions in your factories?

What is your company doing to ensure that its own policies don't have a negative impact on workers? For example, is this something you consider when deciding on a price for the goods that you buy? I am also keen to find out more about your organic and fair trade collections. Will these be expanding and why can't all your clothes be made with organic cotton? I don't like the idea that pesticides used to grow the cotton for my dress are poisoning cotton farmers and their families on the other side of the world.

I look forward to hearing from you, and hope to be shopping with you again soon,

Yours faithfully,

Is it green?

Dear Sir,

A few years ago, I started buying organic fruit and veg. It is important to me not to put unnecessary chemicals and pesticides inside my body. I was really thrilled to find that you have started doing an organic cotton collection in your Oxford Street branch. The clothes are great (you would never know they are organic) and I bought a dress. I am writing to ask you to please extend the range into other areas. I would love to be able to buy organic jeans, organic cotton leggings, and I am particularly keen to buy organic cotton underwear. I really hope this collection is not a one-off seasonal thing. Now that I've bought one organic garment, I am hooked. I don't really want to go back.

I am aware that the chemicals used in cotton farming poison the farmers and their children, as well as the earth, the rivers and wildlife; the pesticides are expensive and force farmers into debt. Now that I only buy organic carrots, I really don't want to wear a T-shirt that has used 150 grams of pesticides to grow the cotton.

I am really interested to know what plans you have to extend the organic collection. Do you plan to blend organic cotton with your conventional cotton? When can I shop at your stores and know that everything is pesticide-free?

Thank you for helping me to be a greener consumer.

Yours in hope,

Of course you might have other issues you want to raise. Plastic bags is a good one. Why not send your carrier bag (neatly folded of course) back to where it came from, with a polite and friendly note asking them to recycle it for you? If enough of us do this, companies will soon start to find alternatives. You may be worried about the use of fur trim (ask exactly what sort of fur they are using, and if it really is a by-product of the meat industry); you might want to raise the issue of recycling, as in what do you do with your purchases once they are worn out? Will the shop take them back to recycle into something new? And what about hangers? Don't get me started! How many nasty plastic and wire hangers get thrown away every time you buy something new? Why not write to ask if there are any alternatives they can use? Katharine Hamnett managed to source recycled hangers for her Tesco range. Tell them how brilliant you think this is, and ask your favourite chain store if they are looking to do something about their own hanger mountain.

It really is best to send your letter to a named recipient, rather than simply addressing it to 'Dear Sir or Madam'. Try to find a name. Go to the top and target the CEO. The pressure group, Labour Behind the Label has some useful names and addresses as well as advice, information and more templates (www.labour behindthelabel.org). If you get any replies, I'd love to hear them. Share them with us at www.greenisthenewblack.typepad.com.

Acknowledgements

First and foremost . . .

I would like to thank my truly brilliant editor, Zelda Turner, whom I knew I was going to have a great time with at first sight, for what has been a hugely collaborative process. Thanks to her the book has a structure, and – I hope – is neither worthy nor preachy. She has logic coming out of her ears (not literally) and certainly more than made up for my lack of it at times. I also thank Jessica Hannan for responding so enthusiastically to my endless emails, texts and odd requests and for setting up the blog, and being such an inspiration (my twenty-something alter ego). Thank you too, to Anna Power for coming up with the idea in the first place, and being so encouraging and supportive throughout.

For bringing the book to life, and hopefully making you want to pick it up off the shelf and read it, Kat Heyes' illustrations are just perfect. Kat's own blog (you must look at it: kat-heyes. blogspot.com) and her book, *Happy Campers*, are an inspiration in themselves. Kat is the real green goddess. A huge hurrah too for Janette Revill who designed the text with such coolness and brilliance. I am also so grateful to Paula Karaiskos at Storm Models for listening, for being at the other end of the email at any time of day or night (usually night), and for putting me in contact with Lily Cole. It goes without saying that Lily is something of a genius – her heartfelt foreword is a reflection of a new breed of modern fashionista with a conscience. None of us is perfect, but I really have to keep reminding myself that Lily isn't either. We need more people like her in the industry, but she is of course, a one-off.

I must also thank my editor at the *Telegraph Magazine*, Michele Lavery, for allowing me to embark on this project, and especially to Kathryn Holliday for being so encouraging, positive and generous with your time. Thanks too to Min and Tony for all your support, and particularly to Min for all your inspiring ideas to do it yourself and for teaching me to make things. Thanks as well to everyone who contributed to the book: Safia Minney (thank you to Arabella); Katharine Hamnett; Sarah Ratty; Cyndi Rhoades; Antoni & Alison; Rachael Matthews and Louise Harries and Rfid the angora rabbit (the fabulous Cast Off); Gracie Burnett; Lovelylovely; Tracey Cliffe at Traid Remade; Rfid Taupe Hynde; Peter Gray; Ed Gillespie; Harriet Vine and Rosie Wolfenden (Tatty Devine); Natalie Dean; Annika Sanders and Kerry Seager (Junky Styling); Orsula de Castro; Georgina Goodman.

I also want to thank and kiss Mark and Sybilla for sharing the writing of this book, not in terms of words but through sorting out my desk and spending so many action-packed weekends without me. I'm back now.